BEST LITTLE TOWN

BEST
LITTLE
TOWN

A Brief History of
Tuckerman, Arkansas

By Wayne Boyce

With a Foreword by
Morris S. Arnold

Mockingbird Press
Newport, Arkansas   2015

ISBN (paper): 978-1-55728-680-2
ISBN (cloth): 978-1-55728-692-5
eISBN: 978-1-61075-569-6

19 18 17 16 15   5 4 3 2 1

Designed by Bright Green Leaves

Edited by Debbie Upton

∞ The paper used in this publication meets the minimum requirements
of the American National Standard for Permanence of Paper for Printed
Library Materials Z39.48-1984.

For Elayne and Edward,
sixth-generation Tuckermanians,
twelfth-generation Americans

"So that things done by man not be forgotten in time"

—Herodotus

Contents

Foreword

Although the phrase "a gentleman and a scholar" is hackneyed, and is often used facetiously these days, it is nevertheless a literal description of Wayne Boyce, Esq. Although Wayne and I have been friends for upwards of fifty years, and so I could be charged with bias here, this characterization of him and his work is wholly dispassionate and objective. Wayne graduated from the University of Arkansas Law School in 1951 and has been what the old books called "a gentleman practizer of the law" for decades since. Along the way, he has achieved many high professional distinctions, among them being elected the president of the Arkansas Bar Association and to membership in the American Law Institute.

But it is Wayne's scholarship that needs to be the focus here. He served as editor of the esteemed journal, *The Stream of History*, the publication of the Jackson County Historical Society, for thirty years. This work required a lot of intellectual effort, of course, especially when it came to writing his famous column, "The Poop Deck," to introduce every issue. But it also required a lot of dogged determination on his part to chase down writers, cajole printers, and rally the membership. It is not every person who has these scholarly and practical qualities in combination.

Wayne Boyce, though he has lived in Newport for more that fifty years, is a proud son of Tuckerman and his pride in his hometown shines through in every page of this remarkable book. If we had a Wayne Boyce in every town and county in our state, our past would, so to speak, be much more advanced than it is. In the pages of this book, the reader will meet many extraordinary people, like Robert T. Dunbar, son of the famous William Dunbar of Natchez: William was a Cambridge graduate, an inventor, the famous explorer of the Ouachita River, and a correspondent of Thomas Jefferson. Less exalted but no less worthy personages will be encountered, too, such as the lady who learned how to tap dance by listening to the radio.

One of the most engaging features of this book is the highly detailed description of downtown Tuckerman in the 1930s and 1940s, which was long ago demolished. This represents an amazing feat of memory and research. Wayne doesn't just provide a highly entertaining tour here: His description will become a treasure for students of Arkansas's architecture and for restorationists for years to come. Here is the Tuckerman of eighty years ago, preserved as a perfect archaeological artifact for all to see.

We are all in Wayne Boyce's debt for his longtime devotion to Arkansas's history.

Morris S. Arnold

Acknowledgments

How is it possible to thank so many people who contributed to this local history of the small town we all love. Tuckerman's annual celebration, called "Home Town Days," draws crowds every year of people who have a special place in their hearts for the place where they grew up or went to school, attended church, and knew some of the best folks in the world. So in thanks, I would include all of those people—some of whom Tom Choate, long ago in an after dinner speech at a slightly rowdy Tuckerman Alumni Association Dinner, jokingly called the "Tuckermaniacs."

Everyone I asked for help in writing this book gave freely their aid and assistance, but a few like Vickie Williams have been staunch helpers in running down so many of the facts and figures. Vickie has hunted down photographs, searched for facts, and been a sure helper in locating much of the material herein. Without her, this book would not have been nearly as complete a story of our town.

Many people shared the family history they had collected and saved. Wes Shaver, whose family's connection with Tuckerman is so long and important, related to me the way the Shaver family tied in with the history of Tuckerman in an almost biblical recital of pioneering and migration. Ralph Smith Jr. turned out to be the family historian of the Smith family. Annabelle Smith Province directed me to him when I asked her for help. Bob Penix was similarly helpful about the Lindley family. The amazing letter written by her great-grandfather that Gertrude Graham Lacy shared with me when I was editing *The Stream of History* is an outstanding piece of Tuckerman history. Gertrude's sister, Lynn Graham Thomas, who is quoted repeatedly in the book, has a sharp and remarkable memory about long past local events, and those memories brighten the stories here. Tommy Choate and his sister Sally Choate Molleston dug back in their family archives for facts about Tom Choate and Community TV. Al Bray helped me write about Citizens Light and Power. Dewey Henderson secured a list of all the Church of Christ ministers for me, and Dr. Joel Anderson, chancellor of the University of Arkansas at Little Rock, helped me find the background of the church. But it was Monika Prysock who supplied the treasure trove of information about the early days of the Church of Christ. At my visit to her home in south Tuckerman inquiring about church history, she went to the bottom drawer of her bureau and produced the archives of the church all the way back to the beginning. She graciously let me borrow all of those records, but kept close tabs on me until I returned them, just as she should. Those original records really deserve a better repository, but they couldn't have a more conscientious custodian.

Two Newport friends, Charlotte and Frank Plegge, have been of inestimable help in locating pictures and getting them in printable form for the book. Charlotte and Frank were two of the group who saved the Jackson County Historical Society collection from the Jacksonport Courthouse when it blew away in the tornado of 1997. Many of the illustrations herein are thanks to their good work. Especially do I thank Frank Plegge for his masterful skill with reproducing photos. The picture "Tuckerman in Early Days" existed only in a two-by-three-foot version. Frank used his skill and ability to re-photograph and print it as an 8 x 10 so it could be used here.

In the beginning of the five-year work on this project, I frequently went to the late James Logan Morgan for help. James Logan was a walking source of local history. I never found him to be in error, and seldom did I find him to be without the answer I sought.

Dr. Jennifer Methvin, academic chancellor at the University of Arkansas at Hope, managed to find time in her busy schedule to read parts of the book and give advice and encouragement. Jennifer has taught me most of what I know about writing and has been my unfailing friend, helper, and muse for many years.

Lastly, there is no way to express my gratitude to Deborah Upton, my editor. A friend of mine from the University of Arkansas was visiting me when I was almost in despair about putting all the material I had collected and written into publishable form. My friend, Dani Porter-Lansky, went back to Fayetteville and found me an editor. Debbie has been my friend, encourager, advisor, and editor. Many of the ideas herein had their start with her. She has pointed out weaknesses and shored up the strengths. Debbie is a most remarkable person. When I met her, she was living alone in a house she largely built with her own hands on top of Rose Mountain in Madison County with the birds and squirrels and the most beautiful scenery in Arkansas. If this sounds remote, it is, but with the magic of the computer, we have stayed in contact and put this book together. I edited *The Stream of History* for over twenty-five years, so I know from personal experience how great her contribution to this book really is. Thank you, Debbie.

BEST LITTLE TOWN

INTRODUCTION

I was born in Tuckerman in 1926, the year before Lindberg flew across the Atlantic, and I have lived in this county all my life save only for a few years in the army in the South Pacific in WWII and a few more years at the University of Arkansas. I came home to practice law, married, had two wonderful children, and practiced law in Tuckerman and Newport until 1992 when the U of A Law faculty invited me to join them in Fayetteville, teach in the university, and establish a legal clinic. My son, Edward, took over my law practice when I went to Fayetteville. When I returned, my clients seemed happy and I went "Of Counsel." I had written a lot of legal briefs, contracts, memos, and letters, but I had never written anything for publication.

Some citizens in Tuckerman undertook to preserve their history by digitizing all the old photographs, home movies, and documents they could find. They also got the equipment to take visual and oral histories of some of the senior citizens. After all that hard work, I thought they deserved a book. I had no idea what I was getting into. I have been researching and writing now for over five years.

I have used *Best Little Town* as the book title because that was the way one of my father's employees at the Planters Gin, Dee Kennedy, always referred to Tuckerman. Presented here is a lot of history that would otherwise be lost if not for the hard work of a number of Tuckerman's citizens. I have made every effort to be accurate, but long experience has taught me that errors are like mosquitoes and just as annoying. I hope you will generously overlook any mistakes in the following and know they were unintentional goofs and not made in malice.

I.

Tuckerman's Beginnings

CHAPTER I

THE GREAT SOUTHWEST TRAIL

Tuckerman, Arkansas, is on an old trail. Indian arrowheads still turn up in freshly plowed fields after a rain. When the Indians who shot those arrows hunted here, it was already an old trail made by animals foraging for food. When the pioneers began to settle in this area in the nineteenth century, the trail was here. It was called the Great Southwest Trail, and it ran from the mouth of the Ohio River to the plains of Texas. In 1860, it was the route the Cairo & Fulton Railroad chose to lay its tracks from St. Louis, Missouri, to Texarkana, Arkansas.

All trails begin as animal trails. Deer, bear, and buffalo foraged along here looking for food and shelter. Their bodies pushed the bushes aside as they ate the grasses, berries, and sometimes one another, no doubt. Their hooves broke down the brush as they walked. They made an open way, and the Indian hunters followed this path, their mocasins packing the dirt, widening the trail, marking it, and leaving the stone tips of their arrows everywhere along the Great Southwest Trail.

The old trail didn't go in a straight line like the railroad that was built much later. Early explorers who wrote reports talked about how it meandered around, sometimes for miles, but it always moved generally toward the southwest.

The prehistoric evidence is scant, but not lacking. Ten or twelve thousand years ago there were people in the region of Tuckerman. They were the earliest immigrants to America. Most archeologists and historians agree that about 13,000 years ago people from Asia crossed from Siberia to Alaska over a narrow land bridge that has since been washed away by the melting ice of the last Ice Age. In 1932 archeologists discovered an unusual stone spear point near Clovis, New Mexico. This hunting tool was distinctive by its shape and the grace of the stone fluting that made it sharp enough to bring down large game. Near Battle Axe, Arkansas, Dr. Joe Williams, husband of Ruth Lindley Williams, found one of these Clovis points over twenty-five years ago. It is still in the possession of the Lindley family. Another Clovis point was among the great arrowhead collection of Stephen J. and Gustave Graham. Cultural anthropologists describe an entire culture of indigenous people as "Clovis people." It was formerly thought that this culture was largely restricted to the west. If that is a correct assumption, some of the Clovis roamed wide to the east, reaching Arkansas. The fact that Clovis points were found here does not necessarily mean the Clovis civilization was actually in Arkansas. The stone point could have been traded to some other Indians. The really interesting thing to the history of Tuckerman is the known date of the Clovis point. There were people here at least ten thousand years ago, and they were using the Great Southwest Trail. Even among historians that is what is known as a very long time.

About nine thousand five hundred years later, in 1539, Spanish grandee Hernando de Soto and a company of six hundred men landed in Florida searching for silver and gold like the treasure found in Mexico and South America by earlier Spaniards. They spent four years exploring the Southeast. In 1541 they crossed the Mississippi River into Arkansas. It is not known exactly at what point they crossed the river, but evidence at the Arkansas state park at Parkin leaves no doubt that the de Soto party was there. The artifacts assembled at the park, together with the journals kept by some of de Soto's men, certainly constitute strong proof of their presence.[1] The Indian village that was there has been extensively excavated. A small bead made of several layers of glass was found at the site. This slender red, white, and blue glass bead is known to have been made at Nuevo Cadiz, Mexico, during the first half of the sixteenth century.[2]

Members of the de Soto party wrote several chronicles of the expedition. Those diaries today are in the National Archives in Spain, but there are English translations in American libraries. While the reports are sometimes geographically vague, much has been inferred from them. The reference to "the place where the White water and the Black water meet" has caused some scholars to conclude that at least a party of de Soto's group made an excursion from the Parkin area to Jackson County somewhere north of Jacksonport.[3] A few years ago after a rain, a sixteenth-century Spanish coin was found on a path just above Central Avenue in Hot Springs. A red, white, and blue slender glass bead or a small brass trade bell may yet turn up in some plowed field near Tuckerman.

On May 17, 1673, Louis Jolliet and Jacques Marquette began the exploration of the Mississippi River and later reached the mouth of the Arkansas and White Rivers.[4] Less than ten years later Sieur de La Salle and Henry de Tonti built a fort at what would become Memphis, Tennessee, and claimed French sovereignty of the whole valley, which they called Louisiana in honor of Louis XIV of France. De Tonti established Arkansas Post at the mouth of the Arkansas and White Rivers.[5] France lost the Seven Years' War (known in America as the French and Indian War) and in the 1763 Treaty of Paris ceded everything east of the Mississippi to Britain and all west of the river to Spain. France didn't recover the Louisiana Territory until 1800 in a secret treaty with Spain. Three years later in 1803, Napoleon found himself possessing a vast tract of land but short of cash and therefore sold the Louisiana Territory to Thomas Jefferson.

The United States' purchase of the 828,000 square miles of the Louisiana Territory for $15,000,000 was one of the best real estate deals in history. It immediately doubled the size of the United States. The territory acquired ran all the way from the Gulf of Mexico to Canada for a price of three cents an acre. Right away Jefferson sent Meriwether Lewis and William Clark out to explore the new lands, up the Missouri River and all the way to the Pacific, hoping to find a water route to the ocean. Jefferson also commissioned William Dunbar to explore up the Red and the Ouachita Rivers all the way to Hot Springs, Arkansas. Later, William Dunbar's son, Robert Dunbar, settled near Tuckerman and founded the town of Elgin.

To deal with this enormous acquisition of land it was necessary to survey and map the area. In 1815 Jefferson's successor and friend, President James Madison, ordered the United States Land Office to conduct such a survey. The Land Office hired Prospect K. Robbins and Joseph C. Brown to establish an "initial point" in eastern Arkansas by which all other land surveys of the Louisiana Purchase would originate. They chose the Fifth

Principal Meridian and a perpendicular base line that gives Base Line Road in Little Rock its name. These two lines intersect near Clarendon in Monroe County. The north-south line or Fifth Principal Meridian west of Greenwich, England, serves as the eastern boundary of Jackson County. The survey team worked their way north up that line surveying and laying out the land in mile-square sections. It was hard going, as much of the area around Tuckerman was hardwood swamp. To the survey team, the Great Southwest Trail must have looked like an interstate highway. The section where Tuckerman was later located was marked Section Twenty-Seven, Township Thirteen North of the Baseline, Range Three West of the Fifth Principal Meridian.

There were early explorers along the Great Southwest Trail. The French ones left some French names like Jacques Creek, which has been anglicized to Jack's Creek, and Cache River, meaning "the river where we stored the supplies." The town of Cash has also modernized that spelling.

Explorers, like geologist George W. Featherstonhaugh (pronounced "Fanshaw"), engaged to look for minerals in 1834, were delighted to find that old trail had been declared a military road by Congress.

> Entering it we found the trees had been razed close to the ground, and that the road was distinguished by blazes cut into some of the trees standing on the roadside so that it could not be mistaken; a great comfort to travelers in such a wilderness.[6]

Making the old trail a military road had helped it no doubt but not to the extent of making it a smooth, straight highway. Featherstonhaugh wrote,

> If a tree is blown down near a settler's house and obstructs the road, he never cuts a log out of it to open a passage; it is not in his way, and travelers can do as they please because nobody would prevent their cutting it. But travelers, feeling no inclination to do what they think is not their business never do it … Often when a track is established round the first fallen tree another ob-struction shuts up this track, and so in a long period of time the established track gets removed into the woods, far out of sight of

the settler's house … These circuitous tracks are known by the
name of "turn-outs."[7]

During the 1830s in the Andrew Jackson administration, Congress
declared a part of the trail to be a military road and appropriated money
for improvement. Stumps were cut, ditches were dug, and some bridges
were built to make a single roadbed rather than the network of routes
the old trail had been.[8] Traces of the Old Military Road can still be seen
in Jackson County, but most of its course has been incorporated into
Highway 67/367.

II.

Early Settlers

CHAPTER 2

PIONEERS AND SETTLERS

The population of the whole Arkansas Territory was only 60,000 people in 1836, but Congress made it a state. There was a lot of empty land, woods land, fertile and productive when cleared and plowed. The pioneers who came were mostly farmers, and they were settlers. This was a time of large families. The land that had supported their parents was insufficient for the many children to establish their own farms and feed their own families. There was a movement to the west from the original colonies on the Atlantic seaboard, and by and large they moved west in parallel lines. The pioneers from Virginia moved through the Cumberland Gap to Kentucky and Tennessee. Those from North Carolina came first to Tennessee, Alabama, and Mississippi. They came looking for land and they found it—rich, fertile alluvial soil washed down by the rivers and creeks for thousands of years, and covered with virgin timber that could be cut, split, and fashioned into houses, barns, and fences. Most of the people who came, came to stay. The children and grandchildren of these pioneers built Tuckerman.

Most of the early settlers near Tuckerman traveled by boat. Going downstream in a johnboat or a raft was easy enough. Going upstream required men with poles to push or men with ropes who walked along the bank and pulled the craft against the current.

A watercraft powered by a steam engine was invented in England, but for all practical purposes Robert Fulton invented the working steamboat when he got his boat, the *Clermont,* running on a commercial basis

Ursie Boyce

in 1807 in New York. Because the steamboat didn't draw much water, it was ideal for the sometimes-shallow rivers of America. The last steamboat on the White River was the *Ursie Boyce*, which the owner/captain Robert Peal named for his wife. It made a voyage from Memphis, Tennessee, to Newport and Batesville, Arkansas, with much fanfare but ran aground on a sandbar at Clarendon on its return trip in 1923.

The steamboat opened up the Louisiana Territory to settlers. While some had come by horse and wagon, it was a difficult journey. Early explorers saw the land between the Mississippi River and Crowley's Ridge as an almost impenetrable swamp.

John "Buddy" Keel, who lived at Ingleside on the White River all his life, told a family story about settlers coming here on flatboats. A flatboat was little more than a wide raft with shallow gunnels. In Keel's story, families sometimes came in more than one such boat, bringing horses, mules, cattle, and hogs along with them. On arrival at their destination, the big boats were unloaded, dragged ashore, and torn apart so the timber could be used in building houses and barns. Keel's father was Arkansas state senator John Keel Sr. The senator served in the Arkansas legislature in the latter part of the nineteenth century, so it is most likely that Buddy was repeating a family story told by *his* father.

The first steamboat up the Black River was the *Bob Handy* in 1831. Unfortunately, there is no picture of that boat, but mid-nineteenth-century steamboats were vividly described by the most famous of all steamboat captains, Samuel Clemens, who is better known by his pen name of Mark Twain. In his book *Life on the Mississippi*, Twain describes the steamboat of the early nineteenth century.

> "S-t-e-a-m boat a-comin'!" and the scene changes! The town drunkard stirs, the clerks wake up, a furious clatter of drays follows, every house and store pours out a human contribution, and all in a twinkling the dead town is alive and moving. Drays, carts, men, boys, all go hurrying from many quarters to a common center, the wharf. Assembled there, the people fasten their eyes upon the coming boat as upon a wonder they are seeing for the first time. And the boat is rather a handsome sight, too. She is long and sharp and trim and pretty; she has two tall fancy-topped chimneys, with a gilded device of some kind swung between them; a fanciful pilot-house, all glass and "gingerbread," perched on top of the "texas" deck behind them; the paddle-boxes are gorgeous with a picture or with gilded rays above the boat's name; the boiler deck, the hurricane deck, and the texas deck are fenced and ornamented with clean white railings; there is a flag gallantly flying from the jack-staff; the furnace doors are open and the fires glaring bravely; the upper decks are black with passengers; the captain stands by the big bell, calm, imposing, the envy of all; great volumes of the blackest smoke are rolling and tumbling out of the chimneys—a husbanded grandeur created with a bit of pitch-pine just before arriving at a town; the crew grouped on the forecastle; the broad stage is run far out over the port bow, and an envied deck-hand stands picturesquely on the end of it with a coil of rope in his hand; the pent steam is screaming through the gauge-cocks; the captain lifts his hand, a bell rings, the wheels stop; then they turn back, churning the water to foam and the steamer is at rest.[1]

One difference between pioneers and settlers is that pioneers were finding new places and many times going on farther west, while settlers came to stay. Pioneers became settlers when they cut trees and used them to build cabins and barns. They didn't come to build towns, but they had general place-names for where they lived. Those places were vaguely bounded, but they were understood by others. J. Y. Harrison had the post office at his store about two miles southeast of Elgin and three miles southwest of what later became Tuckerman.[2] Because the place had to have a name, he gave it his, and that area was called "Harrisonville." That is the way it is denominated on the 1885 map of Arkansas. This area then called Harrisonville later became known as Hickory Grove.

Kenyon had an early post office and was located some five miles northwest of where Tuckerman would later grow. Kenyon was literally surrounded by other place-names of uncertain origin, like Centerville, Bird's Point, Dowell's Chapel, Decker Store, Bandy's Chapel, and most colorful and popular, Battle Axe. Yellow School House and James Store lay between Tuckerman and Elgin. Many other areas or settlements were known by reference to a country school or church.

Robert Dunbar

In 1832, Robert Dunbar came up the Black River in his steamboat. He liked the country so well that he purchased one thousand acres from the U.S. Government and bought another one thousand acres on the Independence County side of the river from Thomas T. Tunstall for $1,000 in gold. Not many of the settlers were able to come here in so grand a manner, nor to start anew with so much land. But then Robert T. Dunbar was no ordinary settler.

Robert T. was the grandson of Alexander Dunbar and the son of William Dunbar. Alexander was the baronet of Northfield and Duffus, a Scottish nobleman whose family history went back to at least the tenth century. "Dun" is the Gaelic word for "Fort," and Duffus Castle was certainly a stern redoubt situated on the northeast coast of Scotland near where the Lossie River empties into Morray Firth and the North Sea, the sea often traveled by the raiding Vikings of the North Country. Alexander's first wife had three sons, two of whom died before their mother, leaving Alexander Jr. to be the potential heir to the title, land, and castle. The baronet married a second time, and this wife bore a son, William Dunbar. The lord of the manor was somewhat disappointed in William. He was a studious boy and rather quiet. In any event, the rule of primogeniture held that

Duffus Castle

the eldest son inherited the title, so at Alexander's death, William received only $500 while his halfbrother got the title and all the estates, including Duffus Castle where William Dunbar was born.

William took his $500 and entered Cambridge University. Thereafter with a college degree he migrated to the United States to seek his fortune in the Indian trade. Ultimately, he arrived in Baton Rouge, Louisiana, where he made connections with a friend of Thomas Jefferson. William and Jefferson never met but frequently communicated by letter. William invented a new machine to bale cotton in square bales, a big improvement and a profitable invention for William, who proceeded to acquire a large tract of land on the Mississippi side of the river near Natchez, which he named "The Forest." It was here that in 1803 Robert Dunbar was born.

President Jefferson sent Lewis and Clark to explore the Northwest up the Missouri River, and commissioned William Dunbar, who was a scientist as well as an inventor, to go up the Red River and the Ouachita River. William and his party ultimately reached the hot springs near the Ouachita, but before he could complete the work that Jefferson had in mind for him, he died. He and his wife had several children, among them Robert T. Dunbar. In 1832, Robert and his wife, Elizabeth, set out in his steamboat to find a suitable home. Thus it was that Robert T. Dunbar arrived in Bird Township, Jackson County, Arkansas.

He "took out"—that is, purchased—from the U.S. Government twenty-four hundred acres of good bottomland on the Black River five miles east of what would later become Tuckerman, and he bought one thousand more acres across the river from Thomas Tunstall for a dollar an acre, which he paid for in gold.

Perhaps that is when it occurred to him to give the name of his father's birthplace to the new village that was growing up around the Dunbar farm, for he named the place Elgin, the town in Scotland only a mile or so from Duffus Castle. The Scots pronounce it with a hard "g" as in the word "begin," while we over the years have anglicized the letter to a soft "g" as in cotton gin.

Unfortunately, Robert Dunbar did not live to see his plantation grow as he had planned. He died in 1837. His extensive library was given to Jefferson College in Natchez, Mississippi. His lands and property were sold to satisfy his debts. The family of Edmund Taylor, some of whose descendants still own a portion of it today, acquired most of the land near Elgin.

With land on both sides of the Black River, Dunbar immediately realized his need for a ferry conveniently located between his farm at Elgin and his land in the big bottoms of Independence County. Of course, Dunbar owned the steamboat that had brought him from Natchez to Arkansas, but a steamboat would be inappropriate. To cross the river in his steamboat Dunbar would have to summon the crew to build a fire under the boiler and get up steam, load the boat with farming equipment, mules, and tools, cast off the moorings, turn the bow to the opposite bank, and travel less than a quarter of a mile before backing the engine and tying up on the west bank. All of this work would require hands of half a dozen men to accomplish on a steamboat. One man and a ferryboat would serve the purpose.

Ferries had been used since time immemorial. The ferryboat had been paddled, polled, pushed, and pulled across to the other side of many streams too deep to ford, but the ferry that Dunbar built for the Black River moved by nothing more than the power of the river itself.

This ferry required a shore-to-shore cable high above the river and anchored on each bank to a substantial tree. The long raft-like boat was hooked to the cable with another cable passing through blocks bow and stern and a traveler block rolling along the trans-river wire. The forward shackle was slacked and the stern shortened. The current of the river pushing against the side of the ferry carried it across the river to the far bank where the traversing cable was anchored. For a return trip, the ferryman shortened the length of the aft line and slacked the bow, thus making the back of the ferry the front and the front the back for the return voyage. Since the ferryboat's bow and stern were indistinguishable, it made no difference which end was leading and which following.

The ferryman's wheel for adjusting the bow and stern cable was amidship. Each end of the raft-like boat had a wooden extension that was raised and lowered to make it easier to roll wagons and other vehicles on and off the boat. These ramps were raised and secured to join the side rails and prevent loss of cargo while the ferry was in transit. Almost all of this contrivance consisted of wooden planks nailed together in a secure and seaworthy manner, but it did appear to be a frail vessel in which to cross the water.

Robert Dunbar built a home on the high sandy land that was later to be called Dunbar's Ridge, and in 1836 he paid the State of Arkansas five dollars for a license to operate a ferry between Jackson and Independence Counties. The license is recorded as required by law in the office of the circuit clerk of Jackson County.

Boats very similar to Dunbar's ferry were still in operation at Elgin well into the latter half of the twentieth century. The last operator of the Elgin Ferry was Lucille Taylor, who was very proud of her title as captain of the ferry.[3] Miss Lucille, a frail elderly lady, didn't actually operate the boat; that job was done by the husband of her niece, Mary Batchelor, but no one ever doubted that Miss Lucille's authority was as complete as any admiral's.

Edward Palmer

In the summer of 1629 Edward Palmer sailed into the Chesapeake Bay from England aboard the *Friendship*. Edward had been too poor to buy a ticket on the boat. He was there as the indentured servant of one Adam Thoroughgood. The usual indenture agreement was for seven years of labor.

Most white immigrants arrived in Colonial America as indentured servants, usually as young men and women from Britain or Germany, under the age of twenty-one. Typically, the father of a teenager would sign the legal papers and work out an arrangement with a ship captain, who would not charge the father any money. The captain would transport the indentured servants to the American colonies and sell their legal papers to someone who needed workers. At the end of the indenture, the young person was given a new suit of clothes and was free to leave. Many immediately set out to begin their own farms, while others used their newly acquired skills to pursue a trade. In the seventeenth century, nearly two-thirds of settlers to the New World came as indentured servants.[4]

Edward Palmer seems to have satisfied his obligation by 1635 and was granted four hundred acres of land on the Potomac Freshes up a creek between the lands of Captain Brent and Henry Vincent on Puscataway Neck for sponsoring eight persons to come to America. Among those eight were his wife, Mary Palmer, and his son Richard. Edward and Mary had two other sons, James and Thomas.

These yeoman farmers prospered, married, cleared land, and gradually moved west, until seven generations later in 1805 Samuel Palmer was born. He grew up to marry Francis Louisa Means and with their children moved on to Bird Township, Jackson County, Arkansas, in 1849. He is buried in the Palmer-Lawrence Cemetery about a mile west of Gracelawn. Beside his name and dates, his stone reads "Born in Virginia."[5]

Francis Louisa Means was called Fannie. Her sister, Isabella Means, married Robert Harrison.

William B. Means

The Means family came to Kentucky early from North Carolina. William Means and his wife and six sons, Robert, William, John, James, Joseph, and Samuel, moved to an area called the Barrens because it had no trees or brush, just wide-open, grassy, prairie ground. It was near a good spring that to this day is called "Means Spring" near Newstead, Kentucky. There the Means settled. They grouped themselves around the spring and took out the good prairieland and settled there about 1800. They were Scots, part of the clan Menzies. The two patronymics, Meanses and Menzies, were probably pronounced nearly the same way in the Scots dialect. Samuel was a surveyor and assisted in laying out the town of Elizabeth, later renamed Hopkinsville, Kentucky.

Uncle Billy Means, aging but vigorous still, is reputed to have killed the last buffalo south of the Ohio there near Dr. James Wallace's farm in the vicinity of Means Spring.

Isabella Means Harrison

In his will, Samuel left his surveying tools to his son William Bozarth Means. William B. took Samuel's surveying instruments from Hopkinsville to Jackson County, Arkansas, soon after Arkansas became a state. There are several mentions of William B. Means in the records of Jackson County. In the 1830s he was appointed by the Jackson County Court to apportion taxes on the lands of Village Township benefited by the different roads in the township. In an old Oil Trough store ledger, James Morgan found an entry where the merchant had charged to the account of William B. Means the price of one bottle of Black Hawk whiskey. William along with twenty-four other citizens wrote a letter to John Sevier, the Arkansas Territory representative to Congress, urging the construction of a road to Jackson County.

William B. very likely told his relatives back in Hopkinsville about what fine country this was in Bird Township and urged them to come here and settle. William Means Sr. had two daughters, Francis Louisa and Isabella, cousins of William B., who had growing families and needed more land than there was in the "Barrens."

In 1849 Francis Louisa, called "Fannie," and her husband, Samuel Palmer, and their children together with her sister Isabella and her husband, Robert Harrison, and children came up the White River by steamboat to Jacksonport. We know this because Frank Harrison was born in the winter of 1848 in Memphis where the party had been held up by high water on the river. The rivers receded as flooded rivers always do, and the boat brought his family to Jacksonport. Ultimately, they came to a spot a mile west of Pleasant Grove (Gracelawn Cemetery) where they built their home, cleared the land, and farmed.

Robert Harrison and Isabella acquired the adjoining land to the west. Both Palmers and Harrisons were large families by twenty-first-century standards. They stayed in close touch with one another, swapping labor, visiting and caring for one another in frontier fashion.

Harrison and Palmer Families, 1850

Name	Age
Robert Harrison	40
Isabella Means Harrison	30
Margaret	9

Samuel	7
Oscar	5
James	4
Robert	2
Sam Palmer	46
Francis (Fannie) Louisa Means Palmer	33
Mary Belle	11
William	9
Sarah	7
Margaret	4
George	2

Some of them lived in Jacksonport for awhile, while the others scouted for the best land to settle and clear. The girls' father had left each of his daughters a woman slave. Isabella's slave was called Pal, short for her full name, Palestine.

Along with the farm tools and furniture, Isabella brought a conch shell. It must have started out in life on a beach of the Atlantic Ocean, perhaps near where the Means family had lived in North Carolina. It served not only as a pretty pink-and-white curiosity, but also as a sort of means of communication. One night Isabella, finding one of the farm animals sick and needing the help of her husband, Robert Harrison, stood on the front porch of their cabin and blew on the conch shell like a trumpet. Robert half a mile away, at the Palmer's house, heard the call and hurried home. The shell is today in the possession of Sam Harvey Boyce, Isabella's twice great-grandson.

In Goodspeed, much detail of the children of both the Means sisters can be found.[6] One of the Palmer girls married a Lawrence, and their son Harry Lawrence helped Tuckerman grow. Many of the Harrisons moved into Tuckerman, and that branch is set out in great detail in *The Stream of History*.[7]

Sam and Fannie Means Palmer's daughter, Mary Belle, married Robert Harvey. Robert Harrison and Isabella Means's son, Robert Harrison, married Mary Jane Lanxton. All of the Harrisons, Harveys, Choates, and Lawrences can trace their lineage to William Means of North Carolina and Kentucky.

Wes Shaver

Wes Shaver, son of Wanda and Edwin Shaver, was born and raised in Tuckerman and graduated from high school there just as his several siblings did. He went on to become a high school teacher in Wynne, Cross County, Arkansas, and the ancestral home of the Shavers. His grandfather, Wesley Martin Shaver, taught school in Tuckerman in the early days. Wesley M. later became the Jackson County superintendent of schools, but it is Wes's *great*-grandfather, Charles William Shaver, who left a remarkable story of early travel to and through Jackson County in the first half of the eighteenth century.

C. W. Shaver had been born on Sugar Creek in Cross County in 1837. It was his great-great-grandfather Shaver who first came to Arkansas shortly after the War of 1812. It was then the Missouri Territory, but it later became Randolph County. His will was probated in Lawrence County in 1836, the year that Arkansas became a state. C. W.'s father, John Wesley Shaver, joined two of his uncles in Cross County where C. W. was born in 1837. John Wesley decided to move to Evening Shade in 1844, his first trip overland. It was this trip that his seven-year-old son, C. W. Shaver, remembered, and in 1913 C. W. wrote about the trip in a letter to the editor of the *Newport Independent*.

> . . . The first time that I was in Old Jacksonport and through Jackson County [was] in November 1844. Jacksonport then belonged to Mr. Thomas Tunstall. The town consisted I think of a little grocery store, and a blacksmith shop with some three or four families residing there. My father was moving with his family from Poinsett County, Arkansas to the pine hills, then a part of Lawrence [now Sharp] County. On our way, we passed through Litchfield, then on to Elizabeth on White River, then the county site of Jackson County. There were several small houses or cabins there. I went into a little store and a Negro man went behind the counter and wanted to sell me something. I told him I did not want to buy anything but desired to warm by his fire. When we got to Jacksonport, some part of one of our wagons was broken and father stopped with the wagon at the blacksmith shop for repairs. We were driving some 75 or 80 head of cattle, and among them were some milch cows with young calves, and Mr.

Tunstall seeing them wanted to buy a good milch cow and calf. Father told him that he was busy with his wagon, but to go to mother and she would sell him one. He selected a nice large cow, and good milcher with a calf about one month old and asked mother what would buy the cow and calf. She told him that she must have $7.50 for them. He said no, that was too much, and at the same time taking a $5 gold piece from his pocket and said he would give her that for the cow and calf, further saying that gold was very scarce and hard to get. She told him his $5 would not buy them, that she had some gold herself, so there was no trade. I remember that it was cold and rainy that evening and we drove up the Black river that evening to Berkley Ferry, through the rain and cane. There were no houses nor settlements between Jacksonport and Berkley—only a path through the tall cane. There was no ferry at the point, nor at Paroquet Bluff. When we got to Berkley we could not cross the river that evening, so we had to camp that night on the bank of the river in the cane, and it was still raining and cold. We had to let our horses and cattle go in the cane that night, as there was no one living on that side of the river.

Next morning father went to drive up the horses and cattle and told Mr. White, our teamster, when the ferry boat came to cross the two small wagons over and let the large wagon remain until he came. The boat came and carried the two small wagons over, and then the ferryman came to mother and asked her where father was. She told him. I remember the wind was blowing very hard and cold, and he said he did not want to start with that large wagon unless Shaver was there to help them, for he believed that it would sink the boat and go to the devil. Mother told him that if that would be the case she did not want her husband to go with him and the wagon in that direction. So the wagon did not go over until father came when it did go the wind was still blowing very strong and the boat twice came very near sinking, father being in the boat with the wagon. As I stood on the bank of the river watching to see if the boat would sink, I could not help thinking about where the ferryman said the boat and wagon would go. But I could not believe that it could go by

water to that old fellow's place of abode. We got over the river
with everybody and everything safe.

Our home was on the east side of Crowley's Ridge and after
we left the Ridge, the country between there and Black river was
very thinly settled. Very few houses of any kind and no farms of
any size in sight—just small cabins, and small patches on which
to raise some corn for bread and a few vegetables. We would
travel miles without seeing any persons. The people depended
mostly on the wild diversion for their meats, turkey, deer, bear
and small game being plentiful on the rivers, lakes and sloughs
for their fish, which were also plentiful and both being easily
captured. At night we could hear the wolves close to our camp
howling hideously.

After we crossed Black river and got to the hills in Independence County, we found more small farms and people than we
had seen since leaving Crowley's Ridge.

In September 1846 father and I went back to the Ridge
traveling over this same road, and found very little improvement
in the way of settling up that country. After crossing Cache River
we were traveling a dim roadway in the swamps, when we saw
two men coming toward us on horseback, one of them having a
long rifle gun lying in his saddle in front of him and leading the
other man's horse. The man's hands were tied together with a
rope. When we got near enough to see the man was a prisoner
and there was a trace chain locked around each of his ankles,
the chain passing under the horse like a girth. Oh! What a sight
that was to me. I have never forgotten how that man looked. It
was the sheriff of Poinsett County carrying the man to the state
penitentiary. We knew the sheriff. That evening we heard some
gunshots in front of us and soon came to where the shooting was
and found a very large panther cat lying in the road dead. It was
the largest panther I ever saw.

I have not seen that country since that time, but I suppose
there has been a very great improvement there by this time.

C. W. Shaver
Evening Shade, Ark., July 3, 1915[8]

William M. Harvey

The land near Tuckerman, Arkansas, in the mid-nineteenth century was all woods intersected with trails and very few roads. The most-used road went from Jacksonport north, across Jack's Creek, by Berkley Ferry, to Elgin, and on to Kenyon. The number of pioneers is too long to list and any attempt to name them invites rebuke for omission. The stories here are the ones I know, but there are many more.

Robert Harvey was a grown man when he came to Bird Township in 1849 with his father, William M., whom Senator Robert Harvey always referred to as "the Old Man."

William M. Harvey surely stands for the spirit of both the pioneer and the settler. He was born in Halifax, North Carolina, in 1803.[9] (Today, Halifax calls itself "Historic Halifax," and indeed it was already an old town when Harvey's parents came there from Virginia.) He grew up there less than a hundred miles from the Atlantic Ocean.

In 1805 Thomas Jefferson was just beginning his second term; importation of slaves was still legal; Napoleon Bonparte won the Battle of Austerlitz, creating international discord that reached even to America, but none of this greatly affected life in Halifax when Billy Harvey was born. Billy at age nineteen married Josephine Blount, and they set up housekeeping there in Halifax. Their oldest son, Robert Harvey, was born there in 1830. Three more sons, Simeon, Benjamin, and Abner, were born in 1835, 1836, and 1837.

Billy decided to move his growing family west. They migrated to Hardeman County, Tennessee, due east of Memphis and right on the Mississippi line. Somewhere he developed such an appetite for fried catfish that his friends called him "Fish Billy." William R. Harvey was born there in 1843, the tenth in a family of thirteen children. Forty-five years later, in giving information for his biography to Goodspeed, William R. Harvey said that his father owned and operated a large plantation in Tennessee.

In 1849, William M. migrated to Arkansas and acquired land from the U.S. Government in Bird Township. He cut a road to his claim and erected a small log cabin. This was the family home where he cleared land and farmed until 1872.

The Oregon Territory had opened up by the 1870s. Many people were hitting the Oregon Trail to the Pacific Coast, and the pioneer spirit in Billy Harvey urged him to go check it out. In 1872, he took three of his grown sons, Simeon (age thirty-seven), Benjamin (thirty-six), and Abner (thirty-five), and headed out to see what the West looked like. The boys must have found something good because they stayed in Oregon. Billy, however, always restless, returned to Bird Township in 1876 and lived there the rest of his life. He died in August 1886 on the land he had claimed from the forest.

Robert H. Harvey

Robert H. Harvey, the oldest son of William M. and Josephine B. Harvey, was born in Halifax, North Carolina, in 1830.[10] At the age of nineteen in 1849, he came to Bird Township with his parents. Young Robert worked on other men's farms for seven years, but in 1856 he bought from the government (entered) the southeast quarter of the southeast quarter, Section Seven, Township 13 North, Range 3 West, forty acres three and a half miles due west of Pond Switch on Jackson County Road 66. He built a house there and planted an orchard. Three years later in 1859, he married Mary Belle Palmer, daughter of Sam and Francis Louisa Means Palmer.

Their first child, Herbert Henry Harvey, was born the following year in 1860. As a young man he became associated with Dandridge C. Dowell in the mercantile and saloon business in Tuckerman. Tragically on New Year's Eve 1881, he was killed in a fracas in the saloon as noted in the local papers and the *Arkansas Gazette*.

Samuel William Harvey was born to Mary Belle in 1865. In the years between the births of Herbert and Samuel, the entire Civil War had been fought. From family history, the war had no effect on the Harvey household. They owned no slaves, and they were just about as far from any military action as one could get.

The third child was a girl named Margret Belle born in 1869. She was always called "Rosie," perhaps for her eternally sunny disposition. She grew up, married Green Choate, and had six children, Richard, Robert, Tom, Alice, Sally, and Fanny. These children grew up in Tuckerman, and in their maturity Richard became mayor of Walnut Ridge; Robert managed KTHS radio station in Hot Springs; Tom operated Auto Lectric, invented the Gizmo, and brought community television to Tuckerman and Batesville; Alice married Hubert Harrison; Sally married Cecil Jones; and Fanny married Clarence Huff.

Mary Belle Palmer Harvey died in 1869, leaving Robert Harvey with a heavy heart and three small children to raise. He subsequently married a Widow Kennehorn.

When he was grown, S. W. Harvey built a big dogtrot house farther west on the Harvey farm, which by then had grown to four hundred acres. He married Maude Harrison. Their two children, Clara and Sylla, were born in February 1895 and September 1896. These daughters moved with their parents to Tuckerman in 1902 where they went to school and lived the rest of their long lives. Sylla died in 1987 and Clara in 1992. Both girls graduated from Ward-Belmont College in Nashville, Tennessee, and later from Arkansas State Teachers College and the University of Arkansas, teaching in the Tuckerman High School and in the schools of Swifton and Newport. Clara married Taylor G. Dowell, and Sylla married Wayne Boyce Sr.

Peter Graham

Peter Graham, born 1795 in North Carolina, married Martha Bowden in Maury County, Tennessee, in 1823. Later they moved to Holy Springs, Mississippi, where Martha died in 1832. They had three sons, Stephen Jirard, Nimrod P., and Jack. Peter married a second time, wedding Susan Pistole, and moved to Jackson County, Arkansas, before 1840. Sometime after 1845, Peter and two of his sons, Nimrod and Jack, returned to Mississippi, leaving Stephen in Bird Township.

Stephen Jirard Graham, born in 1823, married Pocahontas Pistole Greenhaw, widow of Jobe Greenhaw. She was said to have been one-half Cherokee and one-half French. Stephen and Pocahontas were the parents of ten children, a daughter—Cardelia Saphronia, who married Joseph Everett Slayden—and nine sons, Henry Clay, John Randolph, Thomas Jefferson, Frank, Nimrod, Nathan, Josephus, James, and Samuel. The boys worked together to found an extremely successful business and farming partnership.[11]

Frank died very young, but the other eight went on to organize the Graham Brothers Partnership, which was later incorporated as Graham Brothers Company, Inc. Their first farm was barely southwest of what later became Tuckerman. Some of their descendants still live on that land and farm it.

Smith Home

Lee Smith

Lee Smith was a remarkable man, born near Bells, Tennessee, in what was then Haywood County and later became Crocket County, Tennessee, in 1855, the fourth of nine children. He moved with his family first to Gibson County, Tennessee, and then to Jackson County, Arkansas. Smith and his family lived in the Elgin area where they farmed. He was eighteen years old in 1873, just as the railroad was built. He realized as a young man that success for him was in town. He moved from Elgin to Tuckerman and started a grocery and drugstore.

He built a two-story home adjacent to his store. The original store was frame, but a two-story brick building on the same spot replaced it. Known as the Smith Building in the twentieth century, it served as a temporary school when the Red Brick School burned in 1944.

In 1879 Smith married Nora Coe, daughter of Thomas and Sarah Coleman Coe, and they had five children, Gussie, Gertie, Ralph, Kate, and Coe. The Smiths joined two other families, those of Frank Harrison and D. C. Dowell, becoming the third family to move to Tuckerman. Nora Smith died in 1902, and in 1904 Lee married Cora Steen.

Lee Smith, variously known as L. D., or Leroy D., was a staunch Methodist.[12] It was he who suggested to Mrs. Frank (Mollie) Harrison and Mrs. D. C. (Ida T.) Dowell that Tuckerman was big enough to have a church. The three agreed with enthusiasm and commenced work on a frame building on West Second Street and Walnut Street, near the Smith home. Sylla H. Boyce remembered Smith accompanied by his little brown feist dog, Sanko, regularly building the fire in the stove to warm the church before services. In addition to his other duties as trustee and steward, he served as superintendent of the Sunday School.

Elected a justice of the peace in 1884, he represented Tuckerman on the Jackson County Quorum Court for six years. Having learned the problems of county government, he was twice elected Jackson County judge in 1892 and 1894. This experience alerted him to the even wider problems of state government, and he was elected to the Arkansas Legislature, where he served with distinction.

In 1886, President Grover Cleveland appointed Smith postmaster. The post office was located in a corner of his drugstore where he could preside as master of the mail when he was not filling prescriptions for medicine.

One might think it was enough for one man to be a farmer, pharmacist, merchant, churchman, postmaster, judge, and solon, but Lee Smith was truly a man for all seasons. In 1896 he began editing and publishing perhaps the first newspaper in Tuckerman, the *Tuckerman Gazette*. It may have one of Smith's least successful ventures, as there is no trace of it beyond that year.

Henry H. Penix

Henry H. Penix, born in South Carolina in 1818, migrated with his parents to Tennessee sometime before 1825, the year his brother Lewis was born. He ultimately made it to a place near Hickory Grove, Jackson County, Arkansas, before 1851, purchasing a poll tax that year. History owes a great debt to Lyman Priest, a descendant of Henry H., a U.S. diplomat, scholar, and genealogist, who in 1991 began publishing a remarkable story of his family in the *Stream of History*.[13] The saga of the Penix family continues for several issues of the quarterly. It is written the way all genealogies should be written, not just names and dates, but with as much of the stories about the family as has survived in official records, land deeds, private letters, and even in memories and family stories.

Henry H. Penix's son John Columbus Penix was born in 1856 and married Dora Ann Jowers in 1880. Dora Penix was a remarkable person. She was the mother of seven children, and she lived to be eighty-eight years old. John and Dora Penix's children were Jesse (died, age two), Charles, Claud (died in infancy), Samuel, Pearl, Forrest Lee, and Henry Jowers. While the pioneer Henry and his son John Columbus had lived most of their lives in the Hickory Grove vicinity where the Penix graveyard is, Henry's grandsons were born after the railroad was built, and they moved to Tuckerman and became leading citizens. Charles married Nora Yelverton and was the manager of the Planters Gin; Sam bought a farm at the site of Yellow School House on a sharp curve of Highway 37 between Elgin and Tuckerman. Somehow he acquired the nickname "Po Sam," but he became the grandfather of Sam Penix III, who rose to the rank of colonel in the United States Army; Forrest Lee, who was called Buddy Penix or Mr. Buddy by everyone but his wife, Lucy Lindley Penix (who always called him Forrest), and who oversaw large acreages of farmland, directed the Bank of Tuckerman, and managed the Planters Gin; and Henry Jowers, who ran an automobile service station and garage directly across Highway 67 from the Methodist church and married Nell Ricketts, musician and teacher.

While families frequently have long connections with Tuckerman, it is rare that a family name should survive over 150 years, but the rare name Penix has done that. Forrest Lee (Buddy) Penix's youngest son, Robert Lindley (Bob), has both a son, Rob Penix, and a grandson, Anderson Penix, all living in Tuckerman. Anderson Penix is the sixth generation of his family to live in the town.

Jim Lindley

Jim Lindley rode into Bird Township in 1874, his sole possessions being the horse he rode and a dollar in his pocket, but before he died in 1926 he had married twice, sired four talented daughters, acquired large holdings of land and cattle, owned and operated a general store, and founded a cotton gin and a bank. Lindley's youngest daughter, Ruth Lindley Williams, told how her father's store managed to give a colorful title to the Kenyon area.

Among the other necessaries he sold chewing tobacco. The favorite brand was Battle Axe Tobacco. The traveling salesman who called on Lindley was so impressed by the big sales of his product that he put up tin signs on every fence post and tree between Tuckerman and Kenyon proclaiming the superiority of Battle Axe chewing tobacco. People began calling the store Battle Axe, and then the entire area. At first it was said in jest, but as jokes sometimes do, it turned into reality. Lindley, who had the post office in his store, tried to get the U.S. Postal Service to change the name of the office from Kenyon to Battle Axe, but the Washington bureaucrats demurred. Like other place-names in the country, Battle Axe had no definite boundaries. S. W. Harvey lived several miles away from the Lindley store, but his friend and justice of the peace in Tuckerman, S. L. Bogle, never called Harvey anything other than "Battle Axe."

Lindley first married Emma Choate, sister of Green Choate. They had three daughters, Carrie (Mrs. Ralph Smith), Lucy (Mrs. Forrest L. Penix), and Ada (Mrs. Dan Dowell Jr.). After the death of his first wife, Lindley married Willie Gardner. Their daughter, Ruth, married Dr. Joe Williams. Dr. Williams was a dentist by profession but a hunter by avocation. On Sunday, December 7, 1941, he and Judge F. M. Pickens were hunting quail on some of the Lindley land near Bird's Point when Dr. Williams noticed a white stone on the ground. On closer inspection it turned out to be an Indian point. Later study proved it to be a very special Indian artifact, a Clovis point, so called because the first such point was discovered near Clovis, New Mexico. The fine chipping of the edges of the flint are peculiar to the Clovis people, a tribe that died out about 10,000 years ago.

A very early settler named Bird gave his name to "Bird's Point" and later to the whole of Bird Township. His grandson, Bird Cowdrey, is listed in the 1840 U.S. Census. Later, Glass Township was carved from the northernmost part of the county around Swifton, and Jefferson Township bounded it on the south. Village Township lay to the east and the Black River formed the western line. Today a Jackson County road goes west past the old Centerville Cemetery to the Black River and Bird's Point. In 2012 it was possible to drive to the end of the road and walk to the river's edge at normal river stage.

Henry Jackson Dowell

In 1849 the Bird's Point, Kenyon, area was filling up. We know this because
of a most unusual letter preserved over 150 years by the descendants of
Henry Jackson Dowell.[14] Dowell sounds like the secretary of the cham-
ber of commerce of this area, as he writes home to his wife, Ann Martha
Boyce Dowell, obviously trying to persuade her to make the journey west
from her home in Hardin County, Kentucky.

> " . . . I tell you, My Dear, that it is certainly the finest country, tak-
> ing everything into consideration, I have ever seen. It is as hand-
> some a country as any. The land is as green as can well be, equal
> to the Ohio bottom or any other, navigation better than the Ohio,
> and I am induced to believe, as healthy as any portion of Ken-
> tucky, and settling very fast indeed. This neighborhood has plenty
> of citizens for convenience, enough so as to get all the necessi-
> ties of life upon reasonable terms. This county is considered the
> best in the state I am told by those who know. The emigration
> has been greater to this county in the last year than any five year
> period, which goes to show that it will soon be already populated,
> and those coming in now are enterprising, good citizens. The
> first settlers, who are generally of but little value to themselves
> or anybody else, are moving back to where they can have more
> elbow room. I find some very fine clever people here. I have not
> bot any property yet, but I expect to make some purchases in a
> few days. I feel well enough satisfied to purchase without looking
> much more. I think it is good enough for me. The neighborhood
> I expect to settle in is settled already sufficiently to have a very
> good school in it. The greatest objection I have to it is the lack of
> springs. They are scarce, but there is no difficulty in getting wells
> of very good water.
>
> It is my calculation now to buy a small improvement and
> bring with me a small stock of goods. I am very much encour-
> aged to bring goods into the neighborhood. The nearest goods
> to this post office is 15 or 16 miles and I am induced to believe a
> man can do very well with goods here, in reality at almost any-
> thing with proper care and industry.

The climate is certainly more pleasant than Kentucky. It is never so cold enough to freeze the river. Yet it is cold enough to save and make good bacon. Dr. Ives has now as good bacon as you could wish, made since he came here, which was late in February. The weather is now very pleasant, the evenings remarkably so. The musketoes are plenty enough to keep a lazy man well employed when he has nothing else to do. Game and fish plenty. Since I set down to write this I have taken 2 shots at squirrels playing around the yard on the forest trees.

Oh, how I wish my business was all settled up in Kentucky and you and our dear little boys and all were here. However, I will return as soon as I can, but cannot say now when. If I buy I may be compelled to stay awhile to make some arrangements about making some improvements, etc.

You must be of good cheer, and I think things will all work out right after awhile. Kiss the little boys and tell them to be good boys. Also kiss My Ann and tell her how Sweet and dear she is.

Tell Pa that Old Logan, as good as she is, was made after the best material was selected out to make such country as this, that she is too far from home and land too poor.

I will write every week or two. You must write and tell Foster to be sure to write. Yours truly, H. J. Dowell"

Gertrude Graham Lacy wrote:

Ann Martha did come to Kenyon. According to family legend, she and Jack Dowell built a home near Bird's Point and installed glass-paned windows, which were a wonder to the other people in the neighborhood. They were the parents of J. Henry, Foster Boyce, Dandridge Christopher, Junius, and Mary S. Dowell. My grandfather was Dandridge Christopher, father of my mother, Ida Dowell Graham, also of Grace Dowell Holt, Foster Boyce Dowell, Dandridge C. Dowell Jr., and Taylor G. Dowell, all late residents of Tuckerman. The only descendants of H. J. Dowell and Ann Martha still residing in Jackson County are my sister, Lynn Graham Thomas, and her daughter, Mary Thomas

VanWyck, and Mary's children, Mimi and Bronson. Clara Harvey Dowell, widow of Taylor G. Dowell, is the only bearer of the Dowell name today.[15]

Mrs. Lacy's sister, Lynn G. Thomas, remembers the location of the Dowell's home as near Bird's Point on the Black River. The exact location of Bird's Point is difficult to find. It is north of Elgin in the vicinity of Dowell's Chapel. None of those rural communities had specific boundaries. Elgin was that area around the Elgin Ferry. Kenyon was that space near the Kenyon post office where Dowell wrote his letter in 1849. Near Kenyon were other named points of reference, for example, Centerville and Battle Axe. When asked where one lived, people had a range of place choices and usually chose the one nearest their home.

About a mile north of Tuckerman at the intersection of Highway 145 and Jackson County Road 66 was Bandy's Chapel. On north on Highway 145 about a half a mile was Decker Store. Mr. Decker owned a large tract of land at that point. His store was a large two-story affair that stood at that spot long after Mr. Decker was gone. Decker loved horses. He bought them, traded them, raised them, and sold them. He had a lot of horses, which required a lot of attention. He had the money and land for the horses as well as his crops, but he needed expert help to care for and train them. He chose George Yelverton, the father of Paul Yelverton, Nora Yelverton Penix Christian, and Ruth Yelverton Jamison. S. W. Harvey must have bought a bay saddle horse from him. Mrs. Ida T. Dowell had moved to town near the corner of Main and Dowell Avenue. On perhaps more than one occasion she remarked, "I just saw a yellow streak go by. It must be Sam Harvey on Old Decker."

How like S. W. Harvey to have named his horse after the man from whom he purchased it.

The little churches at Bandy's Chapel and Dowell's Chapel are long gone. Only the cemeteries remain. Bandy Cemetery is hidden in the woods, but Dowell's Chapel Cemetery is beautifully maintained by Pawnee Haliburton and Bob Penix.

While these settlers came by boat and wagon, river and trail, big plans were going on in Little Rock where the age of the railroad was about to begin.

III.

Railroads

CHAPTER 3

THE CAIRO & FULTON RAILROAD AND OTHER FIRSTS

Three days after Christmas 1850 the U.S. Congress gave the State of Arkansas a colossal gift of 8,600,000 acres of land.[1] The states had been agitating Congress for payment for their local work that had benefited federal lands for ten years. The so-called Swamp Land Grant repaid the states many times over, but as it solved some problems, it created many others. Arkansas struggled for twenty years trying to cope with the location, identification, improvement, and sale or distribution of this vast tract of land that covered most of Arkansas from the Ozarks to the Mississippi River.

In the beginning, the guiding principle was to get the water off the land by building levees and digging ditches, using the money received from the sale of the wetlands. Amid much chicanery, some work was done, but the Civil War put a stop to the reclamation and sale. The surveyor general reported that in Jackson County 497,741 acres had been designated as swamplands and were therefore property of the State of Arkansas. Today there is only a little more than 400,000 acres in the whole of the county.

In 1858, Governor Elias Conway reported to the legislature that the administration of the swamplands was an excessive burden on his office and pled for relief. As one suggested means of easing his load, the governor proposed that 400,000 acres in the Batesville district be invested at one dollar an acre in the stock of the Cairo & Fulton Railroad Company for the benefit of the swampland fund, on the condition that the proceeds of these lands be applied toward the construction of that part of a railroad extending from the White River to the Missouri state line. This is the very railroad that, today named the Union Pacific, courses through Swifton, Tuckerman, and Newport.

Elias Conway, the younger brother of Arkansas's first governor, James Sevier Conway, lived in Little Rock, a member of a wealthy and influential family, and a friend of Roswell Beebe, who in 1853 became the founder and president of the Cairo & Fulton Railroad.[2]

Roswell Beebe was born on December 22, 1795, in Hinsdale, New York, to a wealthy English family. When Beebe was seventeen, he talked his father into letting him go to New Orleans, Louisiana. He was behind the cotton bales with Andrew Jackson when the United States turned back the British at the Battle of New Orleans in 1815. Beebe was successful in several businesses. In 1832 the *New Orleans City Directory* lists him as a lumber merchant. He also had a brickyard there.

Beebe did not always have such good fortune. The wet climate in New Orleans aggravated his rheumatism. Like many others, he had heard of the wonders the baths at Hot Springs did, and he started there by steamboat in 1834. His physical condition had deteriorated so much that when he arrived at Little Rock he had to be carried off the boat. Fortunately, his friend Chester Ashley took him into his home to recuperate. Beebe lived in Little Rock the rest of his life.

Even before he left New Orleans Beebe had planned to found a town named Fulton on the Red River near Texarkana,[3] but first he might well be said to have founded the city of Little Rock. Land speculation was rife in Arkansas in the 1830s. Many people had bought lots and built homes and businesses without making adequate inquiry about the legitimacy of their grantor. All of this confusion resulted in a monumental lawsuit, which both sides lost, the judge declaring neither speculator had good title. Beebe then cleverly managed to claim title himself, went to Washington, and obtained a patent (deed from the government) for himself. On his return to Little Rock, he laid out the town into streets, lots, and blocks and honorably gave deeds to those who had purchased from the rascally speculators. This left everyone happy and Beebe with a large part of Little Rock as his own.

He and his friend Chester Ashley also gave the public the land where historic Mount Holy Cemetery is located. He served as alderman and for a short time as mayor, established a large iron foundry, and was president of a slate company, but his greatest accomplishment was the Cairo & Fulton Railroad. A newspaper biography of Beebe can be found in the archives of the *Arkansas Gazette*.[4]

There was much public feeling that the railroad should run to Memphis, but Beebe was determined that it go to Fulton, the town he had dreamed of for years, and this determination was the reason that the railroad was ultimately built through Tuckerman. The railroad runs in almost a straight line from Missouri to Texas, passing right through Tuckerman and Fulton. Then the Arkansas Legislature passed an act incorporating the "Cairo & Fulton Railroad Company." At the company's first meeting in 1854 Beebe was elected president of the rail line that was to run "from a point on the Mississippi opposite the mouth of the Ohio River, via Little Rock, to the Texas boundary near Fulton, in Arkansas."

Where, you may ask, is Fulton? It is in Hempstead County on Highway 67 and the Red River about ten miles southwest of Hope with a population of 201. Cairo (pronounced KAY-row) is hardly more significant than Fulton. It is located at the junction of the Ohio and Mississippi Rivers in southern Illinois.

Beebe's death in 1856 wasn't the only impediment to the construction of the railroad through Tuckerman. There was a national power struggle going on between the North and the South. Each side wanted to develop and dominate the vast tract of land that had been acquired by the Louisiana Purchase and greatly added to by the victory over Mexico in the Mexican War that had ended in 1848. This was a matter that was going to be settled by the routes of the railroads. The South favored the southern route that would have avoided the Rocky Mountains, but the North wanted the rails to go west across the plains. The South, if it prevailed, wanted to develop the West with its labor force of African slaves. The North, however, had a different idea—it wished to develop the West with the cheap, white, immigrant, sweatshop labor that was flooding into the northeastern ports of the United States. This heated controversy was fought out in the United States Senate with various controversies and compromises until the northern railroad magnates secured the Republican nomination of Abraham Lincoln, the most prominent railroad lawyer in Springfield, the capital of Illinois, as their candidate for president in 1860. A split by the other political parties resulted in Lincoln's election by less than a majority. The fight moved from the U.S. Senate to the battlefield, four years of bloody war, and a surrender at the Appomattox Courthouse.

Work had been done in the late 1850s that kept the railroad project alive. Interestingly the legislature agreed to repeal its former act establishing the C & F and granted the company new lands and charter, provided the railroad graded twenty-five miles of the road or completed ten miles of track. The portion selected was located between Elizabeth, then the county seat of Jackson County, and Alicia, in Lawrence County. The engineer noted that the stretch contained 24 3/4 miles of straight line and 1/4 mile of curved line.[5] Tuckerman inexplicably is in the very center of this line.

The Cairo & Fulton acquired lands along the route of the proposed rail line and pledged them to New York lenders to secure the bonds they issued. The death of Beebe in 1856 and the Civil War in the early 1860s prevented much work from being done. The C & F combined with the Iron Mountain & Southern, and the stockholders of both companies named the new company the St. Louis, Iron Mountain & and Southern Railroad Company. Thomas Allen was elected president.

The lands acquired by the C & F were used by the Iron Mountain to lay its track and build station houses, switching yards, and watering stations. In recognition of the beginning work of Roswell Beebe, the new company named a watering station in White County for him. Few people today are aware that the town of Beebe is named in honor of Roswell Beebe.

In 1870 the Iron Mountain had reached the Arkansas-Missouri line north of Corning. By 1872 the track had passed Tuckerman and crossed the White River south of Newport. The route followed the Old Southwest Trail and ran in almost a straight line from St. Louis to Little Rock.

First came the engineers and surveyors, marching through the woods, blazing trees and staking out the line for the roadbed, very much like Prospect Robbins and Joseph Brown had surveyed the Louisiana Purchase in 1815. Crews of timber cutters who cleared the right of way of trees and brush followed them. The mule-team-drawn slips pulled earth from either side of the proposed track, piling it up in the center where rock and crossties were laid to support the iron rails laid by the gandy dancers and fastened in place with steel plates held down by long spikes of iron.

The whole operation moved like an army, each crew following the preceding one as closely as possible. Signboards were placed at intervals. Some of them became the name of towns that grew there, while others like Vance remained forever just signs, possibly of some meaning to the management of the railroad. There were signs for Alicia, Swifton, Vance, Tuckerman, Campbell Station, and Diaz.

The old-timers said there was a Mr. Tuckerman who was a surveyor/engineer on the job, and the railroad gave his name to this special place. Years later wise guys in the pool hall would say, originally there were only women until the railroad brought in a trainload of men, whereupon each woman stepped forward and "Tuck Her Man." The joker who made that up probably couldn't put the eight ball in the corner pocket. It is a unique name. There are several Batesvilles, Newports, and Jonesboros, but only one Tuckerman. It has the distinction of being the only one in the entire United States.

The station for passengers and freight was built at the southwest corner of Main and Front Streets in Tuckerman. In those days, all railroad stations looked alike. They were not all alike, in fact, but they were so similar that no one would have ever have had any trouble identifying the building for what it was. Tuckerman Station was not large. It was a long yellow-and-brown painted frame building. The waiting room for passengers was entered by a door on the east side in the center of the building next to the track, just south of a bay window that allowed the station master at his desk and telegraph key to see both north and south—up and down the track. On the north side of the station master's room was a freight room, and beyond that a platform for large freight items, too big to easily put inside the station. In the waiting room stood a large coal-burning stove that gave off an astonishing amount of heat—leading no doubt to the southern expression "hot as a depot stove." The waiting room was divided north and south into two rooms by floor-to-ceiling iron bars. The west side was for "colored," while the east side near the track was designated for "white" passengers.

There were several station masters over the years. The first was W. C. Sicor. In the early 1930s the agent was Roy Congleton. Carl Toler was the station agent in the 1950s. Carl and his family lived in the house Miss Alice Graham built for her daughter, Alene, and her husband, Joe Masek. The Maseks didn't live in Tuckerman very long. While the Tolers lived there, they became the first people in Tuckerman to get Community Antenna Television service from Tom Choate and Auto Lectric.

The photograph of "Tuckerman in Early Days" would seem to be at a variance with the description of the location of the station (see the photograph on page 50). Presuming the street crossing to be Main Street, a corner of the station is visible on the right side of the picture, which would mean the station building was north of Main, when in fact it was south of Main Street. Lynn Graham Thomas remembers her mother, Ida Dowell Graham, and her aunt, Grace Dowell Holt, discussing the point and agreeing that the photographic negative had been "flipped" before it was printed.

D. C. Dowell and his brother, Foster Dowell, built the first general store near the station early in the 1870s. Soon several other business buildings were built.

> The track from St. Louis to Little Rock was completed December 27, 1872, and ticket offices were established at Jacksonville and Beebe, March 8, 1873. Regular passenger service along this route was April 3, 1873. The trip took fifteen hours one way and cost $18.50. April 1, 1873, the Baring Cross Bridge Company was incorporated at Little Rock, and April 14, 1873, the directors of the Cairo and Fulton contracted with the Baring Cross Bridge Company for the construction of a railroad bridge across the Arkansas River at Little Rock. Mail cars began running May 19, 1873, from St. Louis to Little Rock and construction was underway July 26, 1873, for a "freight depot 30 x 22 feet to be erected at Beebe." October 1, 1873, a telegraph line from St. Louis to Little Rock was nearing completion.[6]

Dan and Foster Dowell built the first store in Tuckerman in 1874. They were the sons of the old pioneers Henry Jackson Dowell and his wife, Ann Martha Boyce Dowell, who had settled at Kenyon in the Dowell's Chapel community twenty-five years before and operated a store there.

Legend says the first house was a two-story frame house built by the Dowell brothers so a Negro woman, Maria Lucas, would have a place to live and cook for them. Maria Lucas is listed in the 1880 directory with "(c)" after her name to indicate her race. The Dowell's home was at Kenyon near Dowell's Chapel, much too far to go for a noon meal. The noon meal was the principal meal of the day then and was called "dinner." The evening meal, which most often consisted of leftovers from dinner, was called "supper." This building was moved, remodeled, and worked over several times. Where it was originally located is not certain. At some date it was situated on West Second Street across the highway from the home Jimmy Graham built and where the T-Rex Service Station stands in 2014. Even later it was moved to Dowell Avenue and Main, and for many years was the residence of Taylor G. Dowell and Clara H. Dowell. Before it was razed in the 1990s, it was the oldest house in Tuckerman.

Frank Harrison built the first home in Tuckerman on the corner where the New Theater later stood across Main Street from the City Drug Store. Frank Harrison had come to Jackson County as a baby with his parents, Robert and Isabella Means Harrison. They lived first at Jacksonport but later moved to a farm about a mile west of Gracelawn Cemetery. The old Harrison Family Cemetery is still there with the gravestones of the pioneers.

What Happened to the Iron Mountain?

Thomas Allen, president of the combined railroad, in 1881 sold his stock for almost $2,000,000 to the railroad mega baron Jay Gould. Gould's name exists today as part of the name of the county seat of Green County, Paragould. Gould had previously purchased the Missouri Pacific in 1879. Jay Gould died in 1892 and the railroad passed to his son, George J. Gould. In 1915 the Missouri Pacific and the Iron Mountain went bankrupt. When it emerged from bankruptcy it had been reorganized as only the Missouri Pacific Railroad Company. The Mo Pac was later sold to the Union Pacific Railroad Company.[7]

CHAPTER 4

TUCKERMAN'S EARLY DAYS

"Tuckerman in Early Days" was the title the photographer gave to the picture he took of the village sometime in the 1870s. There is some dispute about what the picture appears to show. Lynn Graham Thomas remembers her mother, Ida Dowell Graham, and her aunt, Grace Dowell Holt, agreeing that the negative of the photograph had been "flipped" before it was printed, thus making it appear that the depot was north of Main Street rather than south where it really was. In either event, Tuckerman is fortunate to have this photographic record that preserves so much of the rough pioneer look of early Tuckerman.

Before the railroad came, Tuckerman was all woods, wet woods in winter. George Palmer remembered years later that it was "a magnificent forest."[1] The railroad changed that. Slowly at first, businesses were established near the depot. First was Dandridge Christopher Dowell, who built his store and went into the general merchandise business with his brother, Foster Boyce Dowell. These are "the boys" that their father, Henry Jackson Dowell,[2] mentioned in his letter home to his wife in Kentucky, grown now to maturity and going into business on their own. In the photograph, D. C. Dowell is seen standing on the porch of his store wearing a derby hat. The hat is extant and in the possession of his granddaughter, Lynn Graham Thomas.

The other businesses shown in the picture from Dowell Store on the left are Alex Lockhart Saloon, Hampton Blacksmith Shop, Dr. Richardson's

Tuckerman in the Early Days

Drug Store, the freight platform, and a corner of the Iron Mountain Railroad Depot.

In 1880, a directory compiled by James Logan Morgan details the Tuckerman businesses and people as follows:

> Bloom, Ben, merchant
> Bloom, Charles, merchant
> Boyce, R. L., MD and general merchandise
> Christian, Riley
> Dowell, Danl. C., bookkeeper
> Dowell, Foster B., salesman
> Dowell, Henry M., salesman
> Dowell, Ida T.
> Dowell, Ocie B.
> Green, Dr. J. M., MD
> Harrison, Frank J., fmr, wf
>   Mollie J.
> Lucas, Maria (colored)
> Miller, W. S.
> Moore, Nancy E.
> Moore, S. T., blacksmith
> Sicor, W. C., telegraph operator[3]

In 1953 the Bank of Tuckerman celebrated its fiftieth anniversary and published some historical facts about early Tuckerman in the *Tuckerman Record,* the local weekly newspaper. Much credit for this compilation must be given to Van Smith, then president of the bank and the grandson of L. D. Smith, one of Tuckerman's early pioneers.

The first dwelling in Tuckerman was the residence of Frank Harrison, father of Julia Harrison Armstrong and grandfather of Otis Armstrong. Julia was the first white child to live in Tuckerman, coming from Elgin at the age of six months. This house stood on the southwest corner of Main and West Second Streets where the New Theater later stood.

Dr. Richardson erected the next frame building on the northwest corner of Main and Front Streets where later Ivy's Cash and Carry Grocery was located. The fourth building, a store, was built by Alex Lockard and located where the Dunn Building stood, subsequently occupied by Deaux Builders Supply. A blacksmith shop was built of logs at the place where the Slayden Building is today.

James Logan Morgan located another business directory for the year 1888 showing a growing business community at Tuckerman.

Chavis Brothers, sawmill
Coe, K. P., druggist
Crow, C. G., cotton gin and sawmill
Deason, George, hotel
Dowell, D. C., general store
Dowell, F. R., cotton gin and sawmill
Evans, Rev. S. D. (Methodist)
Foster, J. W., hotel
Graham Brothers, sawmill, gristmill, cotton gin, and general store
Green, J. M., physician
Hampton, J. M., blacksmith
Harrison, Mrs. Frank, hotel
Harrison, F. J., coroner
Hibbs, James, contractor
Jamison, T. W., railroad, telegraph and express agent
Lawrence, T. E., grist and sawmill and cotton gin

Mathis, J. C., grocer
Richardson, T. D., physician
Smith, J. S., cotton gin and sawmill
Smith, L. D., grocer and Justice
Stroud, I. M., contractor
West, Dr. Crawford, druggist
Wilson, L. A., physician
Young, Rev. A. G. (Baptist)[4]

Goodspeed's history of northeast Arkansas is a treasure of historical data, which must be understood to be a collection of what other people said about their families. It has a certain amount of puffery and is written in the frequently grandiloquent language of the period when it was written in 1889. About the growing town of Tuckerman the author writes:

> Tuckerman, on the Iron Mountain Railway, ninety one miles northeast of Little Rock, and eight miles north of Newport, is comprised of a post office, three general stores, two groceries, two drug stores, two blacksmith and wood shops, one hotel, two boarding houses, a school house, a church, two saw mills and cotton gins combined and has a population of 150.[5]

Compared to Morgan's directory of the year before, Tuckerman appears to have shrunk. Careful analysis, however, shows that the apparent discrepancy is mostly a choice of words, and in reality each report pretty well supports the other. Both accounts bear out that the town had progressed considerably from the small collection of buildings shown in "Tuckerman in Early Days." It was this growth, no doubt, that prompted 37 of those 150 citizens to hire a lawyer and incorporate the town.

Jackson County Court Record of November 1891 records the petition of Thomas Nance and others for an order creating Tuckerman as an incorporated town. It reads in part as follows:

> In the Matter Pertaining to the Incorporation of the Town of Tuckerman in the Jackson County Court:
>
> To the Hon. Mort M. Stuckey

County Judge of Jackson County

We your Petitioners, residents and electors in the County of Jackson, State of Arkansas, Inhabitants of the Town of Tuckerman in Township 13, Range 2 West living in the territory as described in the plat filed herein and not living in any incorporated Town pray your Honor to incorporate the said Town under the name of the incorporated Town of Tuckerman, Arkansas. An accurate map of said town is hereto attached and marked Exhibit "A" to this petition. We hereby appoint Joseph M. Phillips to act in our behalf in this matter. And for your Honor petitioners will ever pray.

The plat appears recorded in the deed records in the circuit clerk's office, but for some reason the early numbered blocks do not appear on the plat. There appears to be some irregular mapping before the lots and blocks become orderly, but this does not seem to have been a problem to the transfer of title for the last 125 years or so.

The names of the petitioners in addition to Thomas Nance are apparently lost to history in as much as Attorney Phillips did not copy them into the order, which he proffered to Judge Stuckey. We can be sure that one of those petitioners was D. C. Dowell, Tuckerman's first citizen, who was promptly appointed mayor of the town by Judge Stuckey.

Mayor Dowell's first official act was to call for an election for the office of mayor. In the election that followed, Thomas D. Lawrence was elected mayor for a term of two years. The attempt to keep things in a somewhat chronological order ends here. For many this book may be only a reference, and it is simply too difficult to search through endless pages to locate the mayor in 1922 or some other particular date, hence they are all listed seriatim.

Mayors of Tuckerman 1891 to 1978

Dandridge C. Dowell	1891
Thomas D. Lawrence	1891–1894
T. E. Richardson	1894
M. G. See	April 7, 1896

Tom D. Lawrence	April 6, 1897
Frank J. Harrison	April 5, 1898
Tom D. Lawrence	April 14, 1899
L. D. Smith	April 2, 1901
W. S. Lawrence	April 1, 1902
W. S. Lawrence	April 7, 1903
L. D. Smith	April 5, 1904
J. W. Sutton	April 4, 1905 (resigned)
Major Moore	October 19, 1905
	(Appointed and resigned)
W. M. Shaver	March 8, 1906
	(Appointed March 13, 1906)
S. F. Anderson	March 3, 1906

With no record to enlighten the researcher, one must conclude there was some sort of political brouhaha of considerable virulence going on in 1905 and 1906. Thereafter peace apparently was restored as the following mayors were elected and served.

S. F. Anderson	April 2, 1907
S. F. Anderson	April 7, 1908
George W. Yelverton	April 6, 1909
George W. Yelverton	April 5, 1910
L. D. Smith	April 7, 1911
G. W. Yelverton	December 2, 1911
	(died in office)
M. F. Moore	February 12, 1912
	("remarks—Vice Yelverton")
W. S. Lawrence	March 3, 1913
	("in lieu of S. T. Anderson deceased")
W. S. Lawrence	April 9, 1913
M. G. See	May 2, 1914
Tad Bradley	April 3, 1915
M. F. Moore	April 12, 1916
J. E. Brown	April 11, 1917
S. L. Bogle	January 7, 1918
J. N. Hout	April 9, 1918

C. B. Coe	April 1, 1919
C. B. Coe	April 6, 1920
Judson N. Hout	1921–1923
W. S. Lawrence	1924–1926
Judson N. Hout	1926–1931
Foster B. Dowell	1931–1933
Judson N. Hout	1933–1935
Edwin Shaver	1935–1937
Maurice D. Livingston	1937–1947
J. G. "Jim" Denton	1947–1953
A. B. "Bud" Bailey	1954–1955
Walter W. Crandall	1955–1957
Harry Biggers	1957–1961
J. E. "Edgar" Parrott	1961–1971
George Bradley	1971–1972
Louis French	1973–1978

In 1905, Tuckerman had grown to the point where more land needed to be added to the original town boundaries. A petition seeking the court's approval of additional space was filed in the Jackson County Court signed by

E. V. Holt, D. C. Dowell, R. F. Dunn, Sam Swann, W. H. Landers, J. R. Yelverton, F. W. Hargroves, S. W. Harvey, T. J. Klais, Mary J. Hogan, S. L. Bogle, Geo. W. Yelverton, Major F. Moore, E. D. Gardner, R. L. Hurley, L. T. Slayden

who represented to the court that they were a majority of the real estate owners of the land surrounding Tuckerman. They designated George W. Yelverton to act for them in presenting the petition to the October term of the court in 1905.

IV.

Churches and Schools

CHAPTER 5

THE METHODIST CHURCH

For most of the first hundred years, there were three churches in Tuckerman: the Methodist, the Baptist, and the Church of Christ.

The first church in Tuckerman was the Methodist Church.[1] L. D. Smith, Tuckerman pharmacist and merchant, broached the matter to two prominent women in the town, Mollie (Mrs. Frank) Harrison and Ida (Mrs. Dandridge) Dowell. The ladies were in agreement and began work to find others who wanted a church and to raise money.

They chose the southeast corner of Walnut and West Second Streets as the site for the church and a parsonage for the minister. James T. Henry and Amanda Brown owned the land and sold it to the church for $50. The church trustees elected to hold the property of the church were I. M. Conditt and G. A. Jowers. Lee D. Smith succeeded Jowers as trustee before the Henderson family gave the lot to the immediate east to "the Episcopal Methodist Church South." Before the Civil War in disagreement over the matter of slavery, the Methodist Church divided into "North" and "South" denominations, a matter not changed until 1939 when both reunited as the Methodist Church.

The church was a frame building located just east of the parsonage facing Walnut Street approximately where the church is presently located (2014). The parsonage, on the corner of the lot, was a two-story house very similar to the L. D. Smith home immediately south of it. Fortunately, a picture of the Smith home survives (see page 32). The church was also a frame building facing north. The main entrance was in the center of the building giving way into a foyer. Inside, there was a center aisle lead-ing down to the pulpit. Robert Armstrong, grandfather of Mary Opal Harrison Hanley and Bernice Harrison Brockman and great-grandfather of Scotty Armstrong, built the pews. One of those pews was purchased by Armstrong's granddaughters from another church to whom they had been given and is now found in the entry to the Fellowship Hall, identified with a suitable plaque detailing its provenance.

The Reverend S. D. Evans was the first minister. He came in 1887 and served the Tuckerman and Kenyon circuit for two years.

Tuckerman Methodist Church has a very complete set of records. The names and dates of the many ministers are recorded as well as the mem-bers, baptisms, marriages, and deaths.[2]

One glaring exception must, however, be noted. Clara Harvey Dowell and Sylla Harvey Boyce know that they joined the church in 1908, but no record of this event can be found. The missing entries are probably explained by other events that were taking place in 1908.

The little frame church had become completely inadequate for the congregation of the Reverend W. E. Hall, and he planned and built a splendid red-brick church on the corner where the parsonage stood. The old buildings were moved or razed and construction of the red-brick church was begun. During the construction period of several months, Brother Hall conducted services in the newly completed school building, which stood just south of where the Church of Christ is now located. In the confusion attendant on church in temporary quarters and the myriad details of construction and moving, the oversight of adding the two young Harvey girls to the rolls is understandable.

The red-brick church cornerstone is still visible in the church today. It bears a date of 1908 and the names of those in charge of its construction.

> J. H. Dye, PE (Presiding Elder)
> W. E. Hall, PC (Pastor in Charge)
> **Committee**
> L. D. Smith (a pharmacist)
> E. V. Holt (a banker)
> S. W. Harvey (a merchant)
> J. E. Dunn (a farmer)
> L. T. Slayden (a physician)
> A. R. Anderson, Con. (contractor and architect)

The main entry to the church was at the corner where several steps led up to double doors protecting the narthex. Double swinging doors led into the church proper. An aisle ran along the west end parallel with West Second Street separating the auditorium from Sunday School rooms and the minister's study. The schoolrooms were divided from the seating area by half a dozen folding doors. When there was a very large crowd, these doors were slid to either end and folding chairs placed there would make seating for a few dozen more people. In normal use, the doors stayed closed. The pews were divided into three sections, a center section and two equal wings. These aisles—left and right—led to a dais at the front. The pulpit, a massive pale-oak lectern, stood in the center, and behind it was an equally massive matching oak throne chair with arms. Flanking the big chair on either side were large chairs without arms. The dais was separated from the congregation by a chancel rail and from the choir in the rear by a waist-high purple drapery suspended by rings from a curtain rod. More Sunday School rooms were across the east side.

The red-brick church served the town for forty years, although it was twice condemned as unsafe. Meetings were held to plan for a new church, but first the Great Depression of the thirties and later World War II prevented more than temporary repair.

Soon after VJ Day, plans for a new church became more than a dream when the Reverend Alfred Knox became the pastor of the church (1945–1950). He organized a money-raising campaign and a building committee, hired an architect, and constructed the present new church.

Perhaps only those who knew it before 1949 would recognize the red-brick church today, but it still exists under its coat of gray paint as the Fellowship Hall, Sunday School rooms, and a kitchen. Strengthened, remodeled, and restored, it still serves as a place of meeting and worship over one hundred years from its beginning in 1908.

The names of those prominent in building the new church in 1945 are shown in the cornerstone.

Erected 1949
Alfred Knox, Pastor
L. H. Conditt, Chairman of the Board
Building Committee

M. D. Harris
Van Smith[3]
L. S. Davenport
Harry Wagner, Architect

CHAPTER 6

THE BAPTIST CHURCH

The second church to be built in Tuckerman was the Baptist Church.[1] It was called Pleasant Grove #2. Most likely this is to distinguish it from the little country church that had been located at Pleasant Grove Cemetery since time immemorial, but there was also another Pleasant Grove Baptist Church at Pocahontas and the numerical distinction may have been necessary to identify it differently from the Spring River Baptist Association with which the Tuckerman church affiliated. The first pastor of the Tuckerman church was the Reverend S. W. Abernathy, who was called in 1894. He held services on the second Monday of every month, and his annual salary was $30. At the 1896 conference, Brother Abernathy made a strong speech about strong drink, abjuring churches to "combat saloons, condemn the curse of the grog shop, and defeat the monster evil of dram drinking."[2]

In 1900, the membership had risen to thirty-five. At the association meeting that year, a Brother Borah made a speech on the sin of covetousness. The minutes quoted a portion of his speech:

> Almighty Dollar, thy shining face
> bespeaks thy wondrous power.
> In my pocket make thy resting place,
> I need thee every hour.

In 1903 the church purchased a one-acre tract of land in Tuckerman east of the railroad from T. D. Lawrence for $50 and changed its name to

First Church, Tuckerman. Shortly before the United States entered World War I, the church called Brother S. C. Vick and changed its affiliation to the Black River Baptist Association. Some of the names of members that begin to appear in the records at this time are Roe Tims, H. S. Hill, Tad Bradley, Henry Henderson, J. M. Majors, J. H. Henley, Mrs. Lena Shaver, and Mrs. John Majors.

The two-story red-brick and stucco building on West Second Street was built in the early 1920s. The cornerstone shows:

> E. C. Julian, Chairman, Lee Seats, C. P. Greenhaw, J. A. Strider, W. M. Tims, J. E. Parrott, Treas., R. B. Vick, SS Supt., Rev. O. A. Greenleaf, Pastor

One of the Crawford-Warren articles tells a story about the construction.

> Mrs. (Thelma Whaley) Street remembers her father working with other men of the church to dig the basement. Her father hauled dirt away with a wagon and team, taking it out to what is now Highway 37W, just beyond the Hazel McLaughlin farm, to fill in a low spot for a roadbed. While the men were busy working on the building the women were busy making sure the men were well fed. They brought lunch to the church—fried chicken, hot biscuits, pies—until it was possible in 1923 to lay the corner-stone.[3]

On October 18, 1926, the *Tuckerman Record* reported:

> The concrete floor is being laid in the basement. The basement walls are to be stuccoed outside and plastered inside, thus making comfortable quarters for the congregation during the winter. Heating plant will probably be installed in the near future.

Work on the building continued apace during the remainder of the 1920s, but with the stock market crash of October 29, 1929, and the ensuing Depression of the 1930s most construction ceased. Services were held in the basement, and the upper floor remained unfinished for many years.

While there was no theater in Tuckerman, people enjoyed "Home Talent Plays." Crawford and Warren relate:

> The Fidelis Class presented a play, "The Old Maids Club," admission was 15 cents and 35 cents, proceeds to be used on the building. The actors included sisters Gertrude and Jennye Tims, Marjorie and Alice Kennedy, and Lillie Mae and Alice Cook. Net proceeds were $32.65.[4]

In 1939, the Reverend W. M. Kelley came from Judsonia to assume the pastorate of the church. Workdays were held every week, contributions urged, and construction continued to complete the broad entry steps to the second-floor sanctuary. A revival with Brother Kelley preaching resulted, among other things, with three young men, John Parrott, Lehman Webb, and Garland Allen, being called to preach. They were granted licenses at the September business conference of the church. Garland Allen became a successful minister; Lehman Webb capped his lifetime of service by becoming the chaplain in residence at Parkway Village, Little Rock; and John Parrott went to seminary and obtained a doctoral degree, retiring to Oklahoma after over sixty years in the pulpit.

CHAPTER 7

THE CHURCH OF CHRIST

Raymond Bailey published an article about the founding of the Tuckerman Church of Christ in the *Stream of History.*[1] Bailey was not only a former member, but also a song leader and hymn writer. His article includes his personal recollections and the memories of early members. He reported that Mrs. Joel Anderson Sr. said the Church of Christ began at Tuckerman in February 1921, and some of the earliest members were her father, Hubert Hall, owner of the City Drug Store, the J. L. Parrott family, and Hosea Bailey and his family.

The first church building was located several blocks west of Highway 67. It was a white frame building, which was distinguished by an adjacent "tabernacle." The tabernacle was a large polygon frame with wood exterior halfway and screen wire above. This unique construction let the breeze blow through but kept the mosquitoes out. Summer was a time for revival meetings, and the tabernacle was an answer to a measure of comfort in those days before air conditioning. While its design may have been inspired by the brush arbors of earlier pioneer days, it was lighted and far more comfortable. It was large enough to hold 120 people.

> The Church of Christ in Tuckerman was the culmination of the hard work of two young men, J. L. Parrott and Hubert Hall. After many months of hard work in trying to buy a lot for a building, Hubert Hall personally bought a barn lot in the west

part of town in the fall of 1920 from Steve and Nathan Graham and deeded it to the church.[2]

The quotation is taken from a very rare publication written by Dick Blackford in 1994. In the book Mr. Blackford makes gracious acknowledgment of the great help given him in assembling the facts in the book by Mrs. Joel Anderson Sr., the daughter of Hubert Hall and wife of the long-standing song leader of the church, Joel Anderson. A short piece by Raymond Bailey in *Stream of History* confirms and complements Mr. Blackford's history.[3]

The lot was purchased and contract let for the first meetinghouse in 1920 with twenty-one charter members.

Mr. and Mrs. A. R. Anderson
Mr. and Mrs. Jessie Lee Parrott
Mrs. Barbara Thompson
Albert D. Clark
Mrs. W. E. Christian
Mrs. J. C. Hodges
Mrs. R. G. Christian
Mr. and Mrs. George Brabzson
Mr. and Mrs. W. C. Berry
Miss Cassie Wolfe
Hubert Hall
Mrs. R. O. Norris
Mr. and Mrs. C. E. Teagarden
John Bailey Jr.
Mrs. Zelpha Ross
A. J. Welch

Mr. Blackford cites those on the building committee as Jessie Lee Parrott, T. N. Graham, George Brabzson, A. R. Anderson, and Hubert Hall. Roe Anderson was a leading contractor and builder and a self-taught architect. He built many homes and public buildings in Tuckerman in the early part of the twentieth century. The white frame building had a hip roof and was set on concrete blocks. Plain glass windows on either side of the double front door balanced the appearance of the entrance.

The first gospel meeting began June 26, 1921, and ended two weeks later with eighteen baptisms and thirteen restorations on the sandbar on the Black River about a mile above the Elgin ferry. C. L. Wilkerson of Springfield, Missouri, was the evangelist, and C. F. Hardin was the song leader.

Over the next forty years the membership grew to slightly over 200 members. A new church was built in 1951 at the intersection of Dowell Avenue, Highway 67, and Elgin Road. This buff-brick building of wood and steel has an auditorium that will seat 320 people. A baptistry, a nursery, a cloakroom, and restrooms as well as a study, a kitchen, and fourteen classrooms were included in the new building.

Hubert Hall, Jack Hicks, George McDoniel, and Joel Anderson were elders of the church in 1954.

Ministers of the Church of Christ

1923	Oscar Hays
1925	Lacy Holt
1930	Clyde Hance
1932–1933	Kenneth Tucker
1937–1938	Denton Neal
1939–1940	Flavil Nichols
1940–1944	Norman Vaughn
1944–1946	Aubrey Miller
1946–1948	Austin Tabor
1948–1950	Harry Pickup
1951–1952	Clyde Hance
1953–1954	Don McGaughey
1954–1961	Eugene Britnell
1961–1963	Kent Harrell
1963–1968	Raymond Harville
1968–1972	Earl Kimbrough
1972–1975	Max Tice
1977–1979	Burl Young Jr.
1978–1985	Jack Gilliland
1985–1988	H. L. Collett
1989–1994	Dick Blackford

1994–1999	Denis Tucker
1999–2001	Ken McKlemmore
2001–2003	Burl Young
2003–2004	Ron Eppler
2004	Terry Shanders

CHAPTER 8

SCHOOLS

As the town grew so did the need for schools. Probably the earliest school for Tuckerman children was at Pleasant Grove, later named Gracelawn Cemetery to honor Grace Dowell Holt, who did much to improve that space. Maude Harrison Harvey remembered going to primary school there in the 1880s.[1] The building was located near the old Graham Brothers cemetery lot with their tall monuments. A more recent member of the Graham family says a family tradition is that those gravestones represent the seven Graham brothers standing together looking at their farm.

The building there was doubtless used for church services on Sunday. Burials have historically been made in the churchyard. During the week the community building was used for school classes. The logical and common practice of using one building for both school and church was still followed at some places like Hickory Grove as late as 1940.

The earliest school building inside the town limits was located near the present-day Senior Citizens Center, which is on the site of the residence of Dr. Joe Graham. An early picture of Dr. Graham's home in the Trails to Tuckerman Archive also shows a partial view of the schoolhouse. A better view of the school can be seen in the "Doll Dance" picture, which has also been archived.

Clara Harvey Dowell remembered much of her school days in *The Stream of History*.

Doll Dance

The Doll Dance was the idea of the teacher, Alice Chapel, who had come to Tuckerman from Barren Fork in Independence County to teach school. The little girls in the picture are dressed in nightgowns and caps and holding large similarly costumed dolls. The performers in the picture include Clara and Sylla Harvey and Ida Dowell. The piano player is Alice Choate, who later married Hubert Harrison, seen peeping through the curtains. The small boy standing near the stage is Harry Lawrence, who much later fought with the AEF in World War I in France and came home to be the Jackson County game warden. Judging from the apparent age of the children, the picture must have been made about 1905. The small frame school building, partially visible in the two pictures, was inadequate for the growing town.

In 1906 or 1907 the school district sold the school building and land to Dr. Joe Graham, and he was anxious to get started building his home there. The Red Brick School wasn't built and we had school one year in the old Masonic Hall on Front Street near where August Krivens' blacksmith shop is located. It was a two-story building located between an old two-story hotel and the blacksmith shop. The Superintendent was Mr. Gregg. Mr. Wesley Shaver, the father of Edwin Shaver and Charles Shaver, taught the fifth and sixth grades. Mr. Hunt, the Methodist minister, was the teacher there for a while.

The next school was built in the south end of town about 1907. It was the Red Brick School that stood at the junction of what is now Highway 67 and Elgin Road. The first part of this school was what later became the center of the completed building. It was a two-story, red brick structure with double doors. The second floor was reached by a wide wooden stair. I can remember two of my schoolmates going up those stairs. My cousin, Otis Armstrong, had had polio and wore a leg brace and walked with a cane. His friend, Brian Parrott, would carry him upstairs on his back while Otis tried to trip the students going down with the crook in his cane.

Mr. E. J. McBride taught the seventh and eighth grades. He was an easygoing person and thought everyone was doing fine, but he got in trouble with one of his teachers. He was a married man with two children and he fell in love with a teacher, so he had to go. Then Mr. J. M. Cathey came. He put us back in the eighth grade. He was about medium height with black hair and dark eyes, a very neat man and a very strict man. He straightened the school out. When he gave a test and a student's answer wasn't just what he thought it should be he would say, "Mark it off." He said that the "M" in J. M. Cathey stood for "Mark it off."

In the tenth and eleventh grades Ernest Williamson was the principal and teacher. He taught physics among other things. The only thing I remember that I learned in physics was that the atom was the smallest part of matter and could not be split. That was what the textbook said.

Miss May Davis taught Latin and English in the high school. I remember Miss Davis especially as a Latin teacher because I had first year Latin and Caesar. She was a good teacher who came from Rutherford, Tennessee to teach at Tuckerman. She boarded with us. Mama would take the teachers as boarders so they could help us with our lessons. Miss Davis and Mr. Williamson taught all the classes.

In 1913, I was the only student in the first Senior Class to graduate. It had been a big class in the sixth grade, but many of them dropped out in the seventh grade. By the third year of high school there was only one other student in my class, Lula Graham (Denton). In the tenth grade Vertie Hurley (Davis), Ida Dowell (Graham) and Ruth Yelverton (Jamison) were in my class.

We had the first graduating exercises in the new Masonic Hall. When he was a student at the University of Arkansas, Mr. Williamson had gone to school with Professor Charles Brough, who was later to become Governor of Arkansas. Mr. Williamson got Prof. Brough to come to Tuckerman to make the commencement address. I don't remember anything that Governor Brough said in his formal speech, but as we were leaving the hall, Papa was carrying my bouquet of roses, and he said, "Mr. Harvey, you are shining in reflected glory." I got lots of gifts. Being the first graduate, I sent out a lot of invitations. I have the bracelet my mother and daddy gave me. I have a perfume bottle that Mr. and Mrs. Emerson Gardner gave me and another perfume bottle from Mr. and Mrs. E. V. Holt. My boy friend, Andy Ramsey, gave me a three-piece tea set. I still have a beautiful blue silk fan Mr. and Mrs. Rex McCuistion from Newport gave me. Dr. and Mrs. Joe Graham gave me an ostrich feather fan.

A larger school was planned to be located in the south end of town near the present location of the Church of Christ. Started in 1906 or 1907 only about one-third of the building was constructed at first. A surviving picture shows only one end of the two-story school. The remainder of the building was not completed in 1913 when the first senior class graduated.

The completed red-brick building had wide halls and eight large classrooms downstairs. The wide stairways at the east and west ends led upstairs to two additional classrooms on the east, a large study hall and library on the west side, the superintendent's office at the end of the west hall, and a big auditorium and stage in the center.[2]

Clara Dowell may not have remembered what Governor Brough said to the graduates of that first graduating class in 1913, but she remembered that the subject of her Valedictory Address was "The Education of a Woman."

The Red Brick School served the town for thirty years. In the 1930s some of the alumni organized the Tuckerman Alumni Association. The TAA met annually for a dinner, reminiscences, speeches, entertainment, and the alumni dance. TAA was one of the very few high school alumni associations in the state. Even fewer can celebrate the one hundredth anniversary of their high school in 2013.

In 1943 a small wartime class of nineteen graduated from the Red Brick School. It was the last class to graduate from the Red Brick School.

One night in January 1944 the school mysteriously burned. All that is left today is the Teacherage. The position of superintendent of the school was recognized to be a transient one. In order to attract competent administrators, the planners built a six-room red-brick house on the school campus as a residence for the superintendent. This inducement of housing made it unnecessary for the administrator to rent a house for himself and his family, provided that he would be near the school and therefore have a twenty-four-hour oversight of what went on there, and be readily available to do whatever education required. That house, the Teacherage, was undamaged by the fire that destroyed the school, and it is in fact still occupied today.

In 1944 the United States was engaged in a total war against Germany and Japan. All the resources of the nation had been preempted by the war effort. Building materials were simply not available. This made a large problem for the Tuckerman School Board and E. A. Fulbright, superintendent. The problems were resolved over a period of two years. First, a temporary school was set up in the Smith Building, a large two-story building in the northeast corner of Main and West Second Streets, directly across the highway from the City Drug Store. The building, built for use as a mercantile establishment, had to be modified and partitioned into classrooms. Lack of sufficient sanitary facilities required the construction of several privies or outdoor toilets. Inconvenient, unsatisfactory, and uncomfortable though it was, school went on.

Tuckerman Special School District recognized that it was much too small to support the kind of school needed for the growing population

Left to right: Horace Harbour, Henry Penix, Paul Craig (school superintendent), Fred Paxton (principal and coach), Charles Shaver, Taylor G. Dowell, Gus Graham, Edgar Parrott, F .L. Penix (breaking ground), Van Smith, Jim Thomas, Dr. K. K. Kimberlin, J. B. (Jake) Winningham (city marshall), A. S. Riegler.

of Tuckerman and its trade territory. Small, rural schools surrounded the town. These country schools went only to the eighth grade and frequently had trouble paying teachers for a full nine-month term. The country districts were loath to give up their separate schools and consolidate with Tuckerman. They had customarily held school classes when it was most convenient for their patrons. In a cotton-farming area, this meant school closed in the fall cotton-picking season when the children were needed in the fields to gather the crop, resumed after harvest, and did not recess until the next fall. Summer school had never been done before in Tuckerman. The rural school districts were reluctantly willing to consolidate with Tuckerman, but only if Tuckerman was willing to concede to have a summer school term and the fall "cotton-picking" recess.

World War II ended in August 1945, but building materials were not immediately available. The school acquired a large acreage on the west side of town where the school campus is presently located. The first building was built with yellow tile on a concrete slab. The center of the building

Tuckerman School, burned 1944

served as both gymnasium and auditorium. It is problematical whether this creates either a gymatorium or an audionasium, but it is certain that it is not fully satisfactory for either purpose. Classes started in the new school at its present location in 1946.

Paul Craig became superintendent in 1946 followed by Lynn Sharp. The Bly Story Gymnasium, the Edwin Shaver Auditorium, and the Clara Harvey Dowell Library were built in the late 1940s and in the 1950s. The district's name was ultimately changed to Jackson County School District to indicate the district covered all of Jackson County north of the viaduct on Highway 67 to Lawrence County and east and west from the Fifth Principal Meridian to the Black River.

A small white frame school building was maintained in east Tuckerman for the African American children who lived in that neighborhood. Instruction was provided through the sixth grade. For those wishing to continue to junior and senior high school, bus service to Newport's school was provided. When the U.S. Supreme Court ordered integration "with all deliberate speed," the school board built a much larger brick building, believing it would avoid integration, but such was not the case. The brick building was abandoned as a school and used as a nightclub for a while.

Tuckerman has always been a town that believed in education and strong schools. With the leadership of Superintendent Jimmy Walker, the school attained full recognition as an accredited school by the North Central Association of Secondary Schools. It has maintained its good standing ever since.

V.

Public Utilities and Services

CHAPTER 9

WATER WORKS

Water is common in our daily lives. We are not conscious of how very important it is until it is not conveniently available. Jack Dowell recognized its importance when he wrote a letter to his wife in Kentucky in 1849, commenting on the scarcity of springs in Bird Township. In Tuckerman, water for cows and other livestock came from a pitcher pump.

To drive a pump in a new location was a simple matter because the water table then was very high. The "point" was a special piece about five feet long, like a pipe with holes all up and down from the spear-like point to the top jointing collar. A block of wood of the right dimensions was set in the collar, the point in the ground at the chosen place, and with a sledgehammer it was driven down into the sandy loam land. When the cap of the "point" was near ground level, the wooden block was worked loose, and the first joint of pipe was screwed into the point. This piece of pipe was then driven into the ground with the wooden block and hammer. At a depth of ten feet, water was usually found. If not, then another joint of pipe was screwed in and the process continued.

The "pitcher pump" itself was screwed on the top joint of pipe. A lever handle about two feet long was attached to the plunger. Up-and-down operation of the handle made the plunger go up and down, creating suction and ultimately bringing water up the pipe and out the spout. If the rubber plunger got dry, one would have to "prime the pump" by pouring water in the top of the pitcher, thereby wetting the plunger, causing it to swell and thus enable the pumper to get a suction in the pipe. All of this sounds a lot more complicated than it was. The pitcher pump was highly effective, and converted manpower into desired water quickly. It was definitely a step up from a well, which brought water up one bucket at a time and was of doubtful cleanliness since dirt, disease, and small animals could easily fall into the well.

Much better and bigger pumps could be driven by electric or gasoline motors. The water thus pumped was stored in a tank until needed for the home. These ways of obtaining water were in use in Tuckerman until the mid-1930s. About 1936 with help of a federal government grant, Tuckerman undertook to install municipal water for all. Ditches were dug, pipes were laid, and homes and stores were connected to the municipal water source. The town water pump was a massive pump that carried water up to the tower. Just three blocks south of the railroad depot, the contractors erected a silver tower. The tower is visible from the top of the viaduct five miles away to the south and from Swifton to the north. Like the Eiffel Tower in Paris it became the town's logo.

The big tank on the top stood on four sturdy steel legs and was a marvel of modern engineering to the town. E. W. Boyce, then a town councilman, was standing near the base of the tank watching the men working high in the air assembling the tank.

"Do you fall often doing this?" he asked one of the foremen.

"Just once, Mr. Boyce," he replied.

With the completion of the work, Tuckerman for the first time had adequate water for home and business. Perhaps even more important, it had a series of fireplugs all over town that could put out a fire before a house burned to the ground. Before the water system was installed, the strategy had been to wet down the house next door before it caught fire also.

Tuckerman Slough

Public utilities in Tuckerman might be hard to delimit. "Utilities" is a term that can certainly cover many things, like "the dredge ditch," and yet hardly merits a chapter of its own. Somewhere in this brief history of Tuckerman there must be a mention of electricty, natural gas, municipal water and sewer, as well as that vital and unique public service, community TV cable, which might well claim Tuckerman as its starting place in Arkansas.

The very first thing the town needed to do was deal with the Tuckerman Slough. Bald Knob was distinguished by a treeless hill; Marked Tree by a slash cut to mark a river crossing; Tuckerman's outstanding physical feature was a slough. It ran through town from north to southeast where it ultimately flowed into the lower end of Swan Pond and Parrott Lake on Village Creek. In winter and really wet seasons, the slough covered all the land in Tuckerman from two blocks west of West Second Street nearly to Dowell Avenue, creating an impassable barrier between west Tuckerman and the rest of the town. Since Village Creek was really a slough itself, rather than a free-flowing stream, for most of its journey on south to White River below Newport, Tuckerman Slough had a very slow outlet. It frequently took days before the water subsided and normal traffic across town could resume.

On July 2, 1919, Tuckerman citizens took matters into their own hands. They employed E. L. Boyce as their attorney and W. Bowman and C. B. Ford as their engineers to create an improvement district to ditch the slough. S. W. Harvey and fifty-two others signed a petition Boyce prepared to ditch out the lowest place and speed up the flow of water out of Tuckerman.

A bond in the amount of $15,000 was required by law and was signed by George H. Brabzson, S. W. Harvey, R. S. Hill, L. D. Smith, D. C. Dowell, C. E. Harrison, R. H. Harrison, Nimrod (Bud) Graham, L. T. Slayden, and G. H. Churchman as obligors. So great was the need that most of the people in town signed the petition that the work be done.

Tuckerman Slough Petition Signers

Slayden Bros. by L. Slayden
Will Hurst
Sylla B. Graham
Jennie Greenhaw
T. C. Biggers
W. M. Biggers
Calvin Biggers by W. M. Biggers
Mrs. S. L. Vandiver by F.L.P.
Tuckerman Garage & Lr. Co by EV Holt Pres.
Jackson County Realty Co by Judson N. Hout Secretary

F. B. Dowell

J. A. Strider

S. W. Harvey

Nimrod Graham

W. W. Coe

W. L. Seats

C. P. Greenhaw

Mrs. E. Burkhalter

S. L. Bogle

Geo L. Smith

Nora Penix

Georgia L. Conditt

Julia Hout

H. C. Fish

W. S. Armstrong

G. A. Churchman

W. H. Terrell

J. L. Parrott

C. C. Gire

J. B. Ivy

W. P. Davis

C. E. Harrison

J. D. Ridley

J. S. Graham by James Graham

James Graham

Otis Armstrong

A. S. Rigler

J. E. Graham

W. S. Lawrence

T. C. Biggers

R. H. Hunter

W. A. Hunter

Judson N. Hout

The Jackson County Court granted the petition and created Drainage District Number Ten in 1919. The first commissioners were C. E. Penix, W. S. Lawrence, and C. E. Harrison. In 1931 F. L. Penix was appointed to replace C. E. Penix (deceased). The ditch was bridged where Main Street crossed it going west, and again where West Second Street crossed it just south of the calaboose. Children crossed the south bridge on their way to and from school. The third bridge was on the east side of the railroad where East First Street crossed.

The dredged ditch never had any more elegant name than the Dredge Ditch. Some even called it the Drudge Ditch, and Tuckerman, in the kind of self-mockery that is endemic in Arkansas, made the outstanding event of Home Town Days "Miss Drudge Ditch" when some men dressed up as women contestants for queen of the day. A town in Mississippi annually celebrates by crowning the "Sweet Potato Queen." Some other towns have unusual standards for beauty, but so far as scholarly research can determine, Tuckerman is unique in celebrating a drainage ditch.

The consequence of the drainage was to greatly improve living conditions in Tuckerman. It eliminated many of the pools, ponds, and puddles where mosquitoes had bred, and made passage from east to west possible all year round, although much of the land on both east and west sides of the ditch remained undeveloped pastureland. Cows grazed there, and barns were frequent.

The original ditching served the intended purpose for many years, but by the 1950s silting had greatly reduced the efficiency of the ditch. The Great Depression of the 1930s made most public improvements too expensive to pursue with additional taxes. In winter, heavy rains frequently flooded houses on the edge of the slough; streets were temporarily cut off by high water, and the public began to agitate for commissioners to remedy the situation.

Bruce Higgenbottom, Max Freer, and Morris Crandall petitioned the Jackson County Court for authority to levy new taxes, borrow money, and clean out the ditch. With court approval, the work was done, and since that time the only problem has been the inadequacy of an outlet made worse by beaver dams near Swan Pond and the creek.

CHAPTER 10

SEWERS AND SUCH

Before air conditioning, which didn't happen until after World War II, the two most civilizing inventions on the frontier were screen wire and the outdoor privy. Few alive today know what life was like without window and door screens that let in the air and kept out the mosquitoes and the great variety of other winged bugs. Someone observed that the true southerner never poured ice tea in a glass without inverting the glass with a gentle shake, thus preventing an insect surprise floating to the surface. Southern summers are difficult under the best conditions, but screens on doors and windows allowed fresh air to come in, trees around the house provided shade, and inside the house the bug-free air could be stirred with an oscillating electric fan. By the latter part of the twentieth century, malaria and other mosquito-borne diseases had practically been eliminated.[1]

Indoor plumbing was common in Tuckerman, but the outdoor privy was not eliminated. The privy was usually located as far as possible behind the house on the alley. As late as the 1930s, a sexton was employed by the town to clean out these facilities periodically. Todd Wright performed this service for many years. Driving his small wagon pulled by a single horse, Todd went down the alleys of Tuckerman in the early evening with a lighted lantern swinging on the tailgate and shoveling the waste from beneath the privy and into his wagon.

In 1951, Tuckerman decided to build a sanitary sewer system for the town. Fred Pickens was employed as attorney to obtain the financing and do the necessary legal work. The cost was approximately $50,000. In 2014 that sum would translate to half a million of today's dollars.

I had been working as a law associate for Fred since I graduated from Law School in May 1951. Fred told me he doubted that much money could be borrowed for the project, but if I wanted to try to go ahead. I went first to Jack Holt, a Little Rock lawyer for whom I had worked in his campaign for governor of Arkansas in 1948. Jack suggested I go to Witt Stephens, a bond dealer. There was no one in Stephens's reception room, but the door to his private office was open, and he was sitting on a high stool working at a stand-up desk. He listened to me because Jack Holt had called him I'm sure, but he told me that $50,000 was an awful lot of money and there was no way he could sell fifty bonds for a little town like Tuckerman. I then went to another personal friend I had made while a student at the University of Arkansas. Jay Hill was a bond dealer in the firm of Hill, Crawford and Landford. He said he would see what he could do. He was more encouraging than Witt Stephens, and suggested to me that Tuckerman could form an Improvement District which could issue bonds to match $20,000 worth of bonds the town could issue. This would leave us short only $10,000, for which we could issue Certificates of Indebtedness. These were legal IOU's, but their interest was tax exempt, which made them a little more salable. The Tuckerman residents and businesses were so avid to have the sewer that they oversubscribed the issue. In all of these legal processes it became advantageous for Tuckerman to become a City of the Second Class, in order for it to issue some of the bonds. It was done, but I thought to myself, "It may be a second-class city, but it is still the best little town in Arkansas."

All was not harmonious as the work on the sewer began. Mrs. Lucy Tims Ivy, one of Tuckerman's noted gardeners, had a large house with flower gardens surrounding it. She had beautifully planted and landscaped the front yard and the back yard, and then she had actually planted flowers in the alley behind her home. She was irate with the contractors who were about to dig a pipe ditch in the alley, destroying some of the flowers there. No one wanted to offend her. The workmen tried to assure her; the mayor did no better; the council referred it to Attorney Pickens, who gave as his opinion that it was not a legal question. Ultimately, some kind of agreement was reached and the pipe was laid. That house still stands today in the north end of Tuckerman, but without Miss Lucy's magic touch, the flowers grow no more.

CHAPTER 11

CITIZENS LIGHT & POWER COMPANY

People from Tuckerman attending the World's Fair in St. Louis in 1904 were fascinated by the electric lights. One of the spectacular exhibits at the fair was the Palace of Electricity, an extravaganza of electric lighting. The fair was scheduled to celebrate the centennial of the 1804 Louisiana Purchase. The Palace of Electricity emphasized the distance the nation had progressed in those one hundred years.

Scarcely over ten years later in 1915, a group of the leading citizens of Tuckerman pooled their money and ideas to form the Citizens Light & Power Company with the stated purpose of building an electric light and power system for the town. The incorporators were L. D. Smith, W. M. Shaver, James Graham, Stephen J. Graham, Nimrod Graham, D. C. Dowell, Charles P. Greenhaw, Joseph E. Greenhaw, George Kimberlin, Ralph Smith, C. E. Harrison, and O. A. Jamison.

The first meeting of the stockholders was held at the First National Bank at 7:00 p.m., September 8, 1915. They elected L. D. Smith president, L. T. Slayden vice president, A. S. Reigler and W. S. Armstrong directors, and W. M. Shaver secretary and treasurer.

The Articles show that $10,000 in stock was authorized to be issued in shares having a par value of $25 each. Already $3,200 of the stock had been sold. The balance of the money must have been raised shortly because the Citizens Light & Power Company furnished electricity to the town for over sixty years. Streets were lighted, power was furnished for electric engines and, most important, homes and home appliances all operated from the power transmitted over the wires strung from the poles of this home-owned corporation.

The last chief executive officer of the power company was Alton Bray, who ran the operation many years until it was bought in 1978 by the Arkansas Power & Light Company, a statewide organization that later changed its name to Entergy, hoping people would mistake that for "Energy."

CHAPTER 12

BELL TELEPHONE

Sometime in the early nineteen hundreds, Bell Telephone came to Tuckerman and connected the town to the rest of the world and to one another. The connection to one another was far more important and had the greater use. A long-distance call was an event that cost money by the minute. There are people even today who begin to get fidgety after they have talked three minutes on the telephone. One banker who lived with his large family on the family farm recalled the ceremony of the long-distance call. There were five or six people in the family. Each person wrote down on paper what he or she wanted to say to "Aunt Kate." They arrived at the country store, the nearest telephone, and the father cranked the handle on the side of the box containing the telephone works and spoke into the mouthpiece that stuck out of the box; he stated to the local operator that he wished to place a long-distance call; and he was connected to another operator in a distant city to whom he gave "Aunt Kate's" city and telephone number. The operator made the necessary connection and replied, "Here is your party." The father spoke to "Aunt Kate," then passed the receiver to the next member of the family, who, holding the written memo he or she had made, spoke to "Aunt Kate" and listened to her reply before passing the receiver on to the next member of the family. When three minutes had been used up, the operator came back on the line to announce the fact and super charges were begun. This announcement usually ended the call in short order. The call was charged to the Country Store bill so it was necessary to make a second call to learn the amount the call had cost in order to pay the store for the use of the telephone.

Local calls in Tuckerman were not so complex. There were fewer than one hundred telephones in town. The Boyces' number was 14. Taylor Dowell's home number was 46. The Planters Gin number was 39. All calls went through "Central." One gave the handle a few brisk turns and listened for "Central" to say, "Number please." After the number was given, Central then pulled one of several dozen wired plugs from her apparatus and plunged it into the numbered hole requested. She thereupon gave a vigorous turn to the crank on her switchboard, sending an electric charge along the wire to the telephone called.

Since Central listened to most of the telephone calls made when she had time, she knew virtually everything that was going on in Tuckerman. One young college student even as late as the forties, trying to impress a friend from Little Rock, put the receiver near both their ears then responded to the "number please" by saying, "Central, give me Uncle Charlie." To the city friend's amazement "Central" replied, "Well, he's not at home. He's on his way to the store, but he hasn't had time to get there yet."

Gradually over the years the shape of the telephone instruments changed. Tuckerman felt it was very modern when the old oak boxes with protruding speakers and receivers hanging on a fork hook were changed out to "French" phones with speaker on one end of the phone and the receiver on the other.

The war changed many things in Tuckerman. The army took over a telephone exchange owned by the Hays family near Fort Smith because it was actually on Camp Chaffee land needed by the military. In exchange, the government purchased Tuckerman's exchange from Bell and gave it to the Hayses in compensation. Since the Bell exchange had been in May Allen's living room, the Hayses simply bought the house across the street and moved the switchboard without interrupting local service.

After the war the Hays family sold the telephone company to Allied Telephone Company, a small but growing business acquiring telephone businesses wherever it could. Allied promised it would install a dial system. Tuckerman patiently waited but no dial system came. Demands got more promises, but not until the town directed its first city attorney to take legal action did Allied show any real interest. The young lawyer drafted an ordinance that imposed penalties on every day there was no dial system installed. Allied sent their attorney from the Rose Firm to the next council meeting to inform the aldermen that the town had no jurisdiction to regulate Allied, all that authority being placed in the hands of the Arkansas Public Service Commission. The city attorney replied that the city and he were ready to appear before the APS Commission any time and argue the matter since Allied had breached its contract with the city. The last thing Allied wanted was the bad publicity such action would make. The dial system was installed in short order, and peace reigned.

CHAPTER 13

NATURAL GAS

In the early 1930s Tuckerman was piped for natural gas. This move to modernity came somewhat later than electricity, and was accepted with less enthusiasm. In the first place, every home and store in town was equipped with chimneys that made both wood and coal possible sources of heat. Those fuels were less expensive and handling them was more familiar. The huge kitchen range found in many homes required a skill built over years of experience. How many billets of wood should the cook use to get the oven heated to just the right temperature to bake a cake? A good cook knew exactly when to start her fire, how much wood to add, when to add it, and how to adjust the draft with the damper in the flue to speed or retard the fire. Skill like this was learned over a long time. Such ability would be useless with the new gas cooking range. Many homes installed small, single-room heaters but kept the familiar woodstoves as well.

Gas was quick. No longer did split sticks of firewood have to be carried by hand from the woodpile into the house. Coal was a lesser-used fuel, but fortunes were made buying it by the railroad carload lot, storing the fuel, and retailing it by the wagonload. A half a ton of coal took about as much space as two ricks of wood, and it burned much hotter and probably longer because of its greater density. It certainly was dirtier. Getting a scuttle of coal from the coalhouse into the living room was only prelude to the even dirtier job of having to shake down the ashes and carry the cinders out to the trashcan.

Former lieutenant governor and governor Bob Riley once said he bore scars in his memory, if not on his forearms, from every day after school carrying the sharp-edged split firewood from the woodpile in the backyard to the woodbox in his family's home in Little Rock.[1] It was a children's chore in most homes, and most children felt pretty much like Riley.

Over time, natural gas completely replaced wood and coal for heating and cooking. The trim cream and green Star of Detroit gas cooking stove succeeded the monstrous old black wood range. Ultimately, the floor furnace replaced the radiant heaters.

Mid South Gas Company was the pioneer supplier of natural gas to Tuckerman. Arkansas-Louisiana Gas Company bought that company in the 1950s. Because some ad man thought it would be more suave, the company changed its name to Arkla.

CHAPTER 14

TOM CHOATE AND COMMUNITY CABLE TV

Tom Choate, the son of Rosie Harvey Choate and Green Choate, was born and raised in Tuckerman. After working in the North for several years he came home to Tuckerman in 1939 and opened Auto-Lectric, an auto parts and appliance store. When television arrived on the scene, he stocked TVs along with radios and his other merchandise. The TV station nearest Tuckerman was in Memphis. The only way a picture signal could be received in Tuckerman was by a tall antenna mounted on the roof of the house. Tom engineered an extra tall tower on the roof of his store, placed an antenna on top of it, wired it to a TV in his store window, and provided television for anyone who wanted to stand across the street and look. Programming was poor in the early days of TV. The most-watched show was the wrestling matches.

Carl Toler was the Missouri Pacific station agent living in the house directly across the street from the City Drug Store. Carl told Tom if he could run a cable from his Auto-Lectric tower to Carl's home, he would buy a TV. Tom and his employee, Jimmy Davidson, made the hook-up, and Tuckerman became one of the earliest community TV systems in the nation even though it had only one customer. It was the forerunner of a public utility for Tuckerman and for Arkansas.

Tom's sister, Fanny Huff, lived in Batesville where they could get no TV at all even with antennae. Tom, his son Tom Jr., and Jimmy Davidson flew to Kingsport, Tennessee, to inspect that town's community antennae system. Tom decided he could duplicate CATV like Kingsport's in Batesville. He incorporated Batesville Community Cable Antennae System and installed the tower on the highest mountain near Batesville and strung cable to the residents of the town. This full-blown system is indeed one of the earliest CATV systems in Arkansas.

VI.

Town Amenities and Industry

CHAPTER 15

POSTMASTERS, POSTMISTRESSES, AND POST OFFICES

The earliest designation for mail to the settlement that became Tuckerman was "Pleasant Grove Number 2." Pleasant Grove was the name by which the cemetery was known for many years. The people thought they should change the name to Gracelawn in recognition of the time, talent, and work that Grace Dowell Holt had spent improving the old burying ground. Unproven memory says there was a church and school at that location before the railroad. The Parrott family burial ground lay between the present-day cemetery and McDoniel's Subdivision. Some of the Parrott family graves are in the northeast corner of the cemetery and some were bulldozed and houses built over them. Pleasant Grove would have been a known place in 1873.

The first postmaster was **Thomas B. Richardson,** who was appointed September 2, 1873.

The second postmaster was the first merchant in Tuckerman, **Foster B. Dowell**, who was appointed on August 13, 1883. It was usual to place the post office in a country store.

Dowell held the job of postmaster for only two months, when the former postmaster, Thomas Richardson, was reappointed on October 15, 1883. He continued to serve until succeeded by **Leroy D. Smith** on January 29, 1886. Here again we have a merchant serving as postmaster. Even far into the twentieth century the U.S. Postal Service found it expedient to place the post office in a country store. The merchant simply took a corner from his store that had the minimum amount of space required to keep the letters, parcels, and paraphernalia essential to do postal business and deliver packages, papers, and letters. One person could easily handle both post office and store. When business grew to the point where this dichotomy was no longer efficient, the post office moved. Smith's store stood near the northeast corner of Main and West Second Streets (see photo on page 30).

In the nineteenth century the USPS was highly political. When the political party in power in the White House changed, sometimes the postmaster changed, too. It was not only the party of the president that mattered. Local patronage was really in the hands of the congressional representative for that town. The Tuckerman Post Office changed hands when Democrat Grover Cleveland, in 1885, ended a long line of Republican presidents going back to the Civil War. Four years later Benjamin Harrison, Republican, defeated Cleveland and put the GOP back in the White House. The dominant party changed and so did the Tuckerman Post Office, as **Thomas D. Lawrence** became postmaster.

T. D. Lawrence was a merchant and the owner of a very substantial part of the real estate in Tuckerman. Today Lawrence Addition preserves his name on the map. Tom Lawrence, father of Harry, Lucian, Shelby, and others, was one of the prominent builders of Tuckerman. His mercantile store was on the east side of the railroad. He surely thought the town would grow that way. In the plat and bill of assurance he filed creating Lawrence Addition, he even reserved to himself the right to build all streetcar lines and tramways on the streets. Lizzie Lawrence, his second wife and widow, once explained to the author that the provision for streetcars was because that was the way the property owners in cities like Little Rock had made fortunes.

George L. Smith was appointed postmaster June 14, 1893. He was followed by **James A. Greenhaw** May 25, 1897. Ten years later on March 26, 1907, **Harvey M. Woodard** was named to the office.

Surely national politics played a role in the appointment of **Judson N. Hout** on February 2, 1910. William Howard Taft was the Republican president of the United States, and Hout was the outstanding Republican in Tuckerman. Being a Republican in Tuckerman in those days was no small feat. The Democratic Party had taken over state politics after Reconstruction and there were almost no Republicans. Hout was a jovial man, short, thick set, friendly, and so popular that despite his political party he was frequently elected mayor of the town. A few years later, in 1916 he and his partner S. W. Harvey built the two-story brick store and office building at the northeast corner of Main and Front Streets. The partners' names are still silent witness in blue tiles set in the entrance to what for many years was the Ivy Cash and Carry Store. To gain access to the offices on the second floor required a short walk up Front Street toward the blacksmith shop; there at the rear of the building was a door that granted admission to a stair ascending to the upper level. Dr. J. B. Ivy, physician, maintained his offices there for many years. The front offices, overlooking Main Street, were shared by Harvey and Hout and after S. W. Harvey's death in June 1926 by Hout alone. The reception room was large enough for the Tuckerman Band to have band practice there in the evening by Mr. Hout's permission. There were never more than ten students in the band, but they filled the otherwise quiet downtown evening of the early 1940s with martial music.

Robert Hubert Harrison became postmaster with another change of government in 1913 when Woodrow Wilson defeated Taft and Teddy Roosevelt, the Bull Moose candidate. Harrison had recently married his cousin Alice Choate, and they together raised three girls: Lou Alice H. Battle, who taught school in Tuckerman High School before she married Bill Battle and moved off to Georgia, and the twins, Doris and Dorcas. Later in life he blamed his indigestion on having eaten every meal seated between the twins. Harrison was for many years a partner with his older brother, Charlie E. Harrison, in the general mercantile business. Their store, Harrison Brothers, was located east of but adjacent to the Bank of Tuckerman on Main.

Perhaps it was a coincidence that Harrison was succeeded in the post office by his brother-in-law, **Robert H. Choate**, who was appointed June 4, 1920. Events that may seem to have a connection to one used to a large city may, in a small town like Tuckerman, have no connection at all. Choate later moved to Hot Springs and a career as station manager of KTHS radio station. A psychologist living in Hot Springs had written a book on human behavior. He had a thirty-minute program on the radio where he answered callers' questions on the air, much like Kelsey Grammer's recent TV character. One day the learned doctor was sick and failed to appear. Choate with no explanation simply substituted himself as the psychologist on the air, and since it was radio, no one knew the difference. Questioned about the ethics of this, he said, "Not a problem. After all, I had read his book."

Tuckerman's first postmistress was **Olga C. Roberts,** appointed June 11, 1928. Miss Olga was a statuesque lady who in later years raised her sister Alta Moon's three orphaned children. Her post office was in the Hout building with its entrance on the Front Street side. By this time the post office had two hundred or more private mailboxes secured with combination locks. The mail was sorted and placed in the appropriate box. No longer did one have to call for his mail at the window.

The post office moved again in the early 1930s to a more commodious building on the west side of West Second Street about halfway between City Drug Store and the *Tuckerman Record* building. **Charles K. Coe**, son of county judge Charles Coe, became the postmaster. Judge Coe owned a large farm where Charlie Coe had been raised, located about midway between Tuckerman and Newport. The Coes were a large family with five sons. In addition, their mother was a Harrison. First and last Charlie Coe must have been kin to three-quarters of the people in Bird Township. That is the sort of thing of which any elected officeholder should be aware.

Coe later ran a grocery store next to the *Tuckerman Record*. He kept the monthly charge accounts on small three-by-five ticket books. On one occasion Sylla Boyce paid her account by writing a check to "Charlie Coe" and inadvertently signed it "Charlie Coe." He equally accidentally deposited it along with other checks. The bank of course charged it against his account. He was really ashamed to tell his customer how both of them had goofed. She thought it was hilariously nutty of both of them and wrote him another check signed "Sylla H. Boyce."

Foster B. Dowell was the nephew of the first F. B. Dowell, postmaster back in the nineteenth century. For many years he had operated the City Meat Market. His wife, Myrtle Horn Dowell, worked in the store with him. They were a jovial couple, called Auntie Mo and Uncle Fos by many children who frequented the store.

Myrtle H. Dowell succeeded Foster at his death, to become the second postmistress, serving until she retired in 1961.

William Cletus Coe, who with his wife, Mary Coe, operated the City Café, became postmaster when Miss Myrtle retired. He served until he retired to enter Seminary and become an ordained Methodist minister.

Chronological List of Later Postmasters and Postmistresses, 1961–1999

William Cletus Coe	Postmaster	7/24/1961
Kenneth R. Eaton	Officer in charge	12/16/1983
Tommy L. Reynolds	Officer in charge	4/27/1984
John O. Washam	Postmaster	5/12/1984
Lewis Smith	Officer in charge	
Brenda J. Prater	Postmaster	2/23/1991
Mable Parks	Officer in charge	7/11/1992
James A. Marshall	Postmaster	3/20/1993
Shirion K. Best	Officer in charge	4/15/1999
Theresa Peebles	Officer in charge	5/20/1999
Shirion K. Best	Postmaster	9/11/1999

S.W. Harvey general store

CHAPTER 16

MEDICINE MEN

Before Tuckerman was a town, there were men practicing medicine in Bird Township. The 1880 census records a Doctor William Sprigg, age forty-eight, living with his wife, R. J., and two sons, William J. and James D., in the vicinity of Elgin and a Dr. Rufus R. W. Ridley, who reported his occupation as "M.D. & Farmer."

The first physician about whom much is known was Dr. R. L. Boyce.[1] When Jack Dowell wrote his letter to his wife in 1849 from Kenyon, he asked for the whereabouts of R. L. Boyce. Dr. Boyce was likely a relative of Ann Martha Boyce Dowell. He was a graduate of the University of St. Louis. In 1860 he commenced practicing medicine in the vicinity of Battle Axe near Dowell's home and store. The directory published by James S. Jones in 1880 shows him operating a general store and pharmacy in connection with his medical practice in Tuckerman. Not until 1881 were physicians required by law to register with the county wherein they practiced. On April 14, 1881, Dr. Boyce duly appeared before R. M. Bandy, clerk, and registered his medical credentials.

Also shown in the 1880 directory of Tuckerman business and professional persons was a Dr. J. M. Green, about whom no more is known.

The seven Graham brothers had a sister, Cordelia Sophronia, who married Joseph Slayden. Their son, Levi Tillman Slayden, in 1885 graduated from the Collegie Medicinal Missouraenus, which is assumed to be the Latin name for the Missouri Medical College in St. Louis. Dr. Slayden married Mattie Gardner. They built the beautiful red-brick home standing on the northwest corner of West Second and Hazel with much the same appearance it has always had.

Dr. Slayden was a builder. The two-story Slayden Building on Main Street has a large walk-in vault. There are wagon scales in the rear. It housed a mercantile store on the ground floor and Dr. Slayden's medical office upstairs. He was a farmer, banker, and businessman, and built the building to accommodate all his many business and professional interests. A devout Methodist, he was a member of the board of stewards that built the red-brick Methodist Church. His marriage to Miss Mattie yielded three children: a son, Neil, and two daughters, Louise and Irma.

In 1888, Dr. Joe Graham, one of the seven Graham brothers, graduated from the Medical Department of the University of Nashville, later to become Vanderbilt University. Vanderbilt was originally a Methodist college until a Methodist bishop suggested to Cornelius Vanderbilt that for a million dollars the name could be changed. Commodore Vanderbilt was only too happy to oblige, and the university has honored him ever since by becoming one of the leading medical schools in the South. Dr. Graham married Sylla Bandy and built a house where the first Tuckerman school once stood and where the Tuckerman Civic Center now stands.

Dr. J. C. Kimberlin's father was interested in the timber business and settled in the vicinity of Campbell Station. Dr. J. C. Kimberlin and his son Kenneth Knox Kimberlin followed him to Arkansas. Dr. K. K. Kimberlin was born in Indianapolis, Indiana, in 1882. Following the completion of his high school studies in Newport, he entered the Indianapolis School of Medicine, graduating there in 1904. He returned to Arkansas and became associated with his father in the practice of medicine in Tuckerman. He married Louanna Person and they had two children, Helen K. Henderson and a son Kenneth, who later became a doctor and lived and practiced in Michigan.

Dr. Kimberlin was active in the civic affairs of Tuckerman, serving on the town council and the Tuckerman School Board, and as president of the Tuckerman Service Club. He was also a member of the Jackson County Medical Society and the local chapter of the Masonic Lodge.

K. K. Kimberlin practiced medicine in Tuckerman for forty-eight years, until shortly before his death on January 3, 1953. He is buried in the Kimberlin plot in Walnut Grove Cemetery in Newport beside his first wife.

Dr. Kimberlin's second wife, Lola Scott, survived him many years and is buried in Little Rock.

Dr. O. A. Jamison was admitted to practice medicine in Jackson County in 1902 and recertified for some reason in 1903. Dr. Jamison and his first wife had a daughter, Oneal J. Bjorkman. After the death of his first wife, he married Ruth Yelverton, and they had one son, Glenn Jamison. Dr. Jamison served as a medical officer in World War I with the American Expeditionary Force in France.

Dr. J. B. Ivy was recertified to practice medicine August 18, 1903; the recertification was refilled for some bureaucratic reason June 20, 1916. Dr. Ivy came to Tuckerman from Stone County. He and his wife had a daughter, Beatrice, who married Gus Graham. They also had two sons Bill and Bryan. Bryan graduated from medical school and practiced medicine in Weslaco, Texas.

Dr. R. O. Norris named his weekend retreat at Cherokee Village "Medicine Man Lodge." His office in Tuckerman was just about the center of the block between the City Drug Store and the *Tuckerman Record*. The building had no doubt earlier been a mercantile store since the waiting room across the front was separated from the passing public on the sidewalk by only large plate-glass windows. One of the charms of a small town was its lack of privacy. Everyone knew everything about everybody.

Mrs. Nora (McCartney) Norris presided over the waiting room, answered the telephone, and kept the books. The very neat books were of her own devising but show that Dr. Norris was seeing dozens of patients a day for a fee of one dollar for an office call, many of which were charged to the patient's account. Cash money was very scarce in June 1930 in Tuckerman. The daybook in the possession of the author running from June 1930 to October 1931 is a historical treasure of the names and the times in the Great Depression. Apparently no one was turned away for lack of funds, and a great deal of the debt must have been paid in chickens and eggs. Dr. Norris graduated from the Eclectic School of Medicine in Kansas City in 1909, and practiced for a time in Sharp County and at Auvergne before coming to Tuckerman in 1912. He and Mrs. Norris had one daughter, Carma Francine, who married Bill Cate, founder of radio and TV station KAIT in Jonesboro.

Dr. Harry E. Dowell graduated from dental college and in 1904 was certified by the Jackson County Board of Examiners to practice dentistry.

Dr. Dowell practiced for a time in Tuckerman but soon left to begin a new practice in St. Louis. (To this day in 2014, Tuckerman has not had another dentist.) He married Mable Dowell, who was teaching school at Battle Axe about 1899. Clara Harvey Dowell was one of her students and forever remembered Miss Mable insisting that Dr. Dowell drive young Clara to her home before the couple drove on to Newport to get married.

In the 1930s Tuckerman had a population of fewer than 1,000 people served by Doctors Kimberlin, Norris, Jamison, Slayden, and Ivy. These men had all come in the early years of the century. They were dying out by the middle of the century. The younger doctors coming out of school in the 1950s had been trained to hospital practice, and without a hospital in Tuckerman it was difficult to get or keep physicians.

About 1950 a concerted effort was made to get some young doctors to settle in Tuckerman. L. F. Farmer, president of the First National Bank, was largely responsible for persuading Dean Werner and Ed Novak to open their practice in Tuckerman. Medical education had changed. Medical students were trained to practice with a hospital rather than in their offices or by making house calls. Doctors Werner and Novak were warmly received in Tuckerman, but the inconvenience of making case rounds on their patients in the Newport Hospital soon caused them to go elsewhere and Tuckerman was again without a doctor.

The day of the house call and the doctor's "black bag" were over and medicine moved to Newport.

CHAPTER 17

COTTON GINS, SAWMILLS, AND ICE PLANTS

Tuckerman was a market town, a place to buy and sell. It served with goods and services the rich farming hinterland that surrounded it. The few businesses that could qualify as "industry" were incidental but appropriate to farming. Industry usually makes things for export. Cotton gins bought and processed the cotton crop and sold the baled cotton to Newport cotton buyers who represented cotton companies in Memphis. The sawmill turned the logs into crossties for the railroads and boards and beams for houses and shops wherever they were needed.

The Crystal Ice Plant didn't export its product. It made huge one-hundred-pound blocks of ice for local consumption. It was a luxury product that served the town folk and kept their perishables fresh longer, cooled their ice tea, and chilled their watermelons. Some ice was sold right from the plant located at the north end of East First Street just past the Planters Gin and the Seay Row. The business belonged to H. E. James of Elgin, but Hub James was seldom seen at the ice plant. Lewis Hartman appeared to run the entire operation. A "dime's worth of ice" was all that was needed for a freezer of ice cream. A high platform fronted the plant and storage room with a small office at the north end. Hartman appeared from the office, opened the heavy door, and with his ice pick chiseled off about ten pounds from a larger block. Then with his ice tongs, he lifted it and carried it to the front bumper of the customer's car.

Hartman daily delivered ice from a one-horse wagon. A canvas wagon sheet covered the ice to slow the melting. Most kept the refrigerator on the back porch. Hartman chiseled off the required amount from the bigger blocks in the wagon, hooked the piece to be delivered with his ice tongs, hoisted it on his shoulder, and carried it to the icebox on the back porch. He never objected to the children who followed the ice wagon, eating the little pieces of ice that had chipped away.

After the war (World War II), James realized the old plant was obsolete and built a new, state-of-the-art ice plant where the U.S. Post Office now stands near the northwest corner of Front and Hazel Streets. Unfortunately for the ice manufacturing business, home freezers and electric refrigerators soon made even the new ice plant redundant.

In a business directory published in 1880 by James S. Jones, Tuckerman is referred to as a village, while Jacksonport, Newport, and Grand Glaize are all denominated "towns." Jones shows the only few businesses in Tuckerman as three merchants and a blacksmith.

Myrtle Farmer Gaddy in her book *Charles Pistole and His Descendants* tells how the Graham brothers got into business.

> Henry Clay Graham … [and] two of his brothers John [York] Graham and Thomas Jefferson Graham began to acquire and operate additional farm land as a partnership. In 1880, these three brothers opened a mercantile business under the name of Graham Brothers. As the younger brothers came of age, they were taken into the firm and by 1890 all eight Graham brothers were partners in the mercantile business, farming operations and other enterprises. The firm built a cotton gin in Tuckerman in 1880. Graham Brothers Company was incorporated in 1903 with the surviving seven brothers. [Samuel was deceased in 1899.] Thomas J. Graham was the president, James Graham was vice president and Nathan was secretary and treasurer. The Articles of Incorporation stated the purposes of the Company: "to engage in farming and carry on a general mercantile trading business which shall include the buying and selling of all kinds of goods, wares, merchandise and such articles and products and commodities as usually bought and sold in the vicinity which shall include cotton, live stock of all kinds and to own and oper-

ate cotton gins and presses and saw mills." Henry Clay Graham died in 1904 of a heart attack while he was enroute to his home on the farm, a little less than a mile west of Tuckerman where the Grahams first settled. The above listed activities were carried on by the brothers.[1]

There is a reference in Goodspeed to "two gins and sawmills combined" in Tuckerman in 1889; one of those was, of course, the Graham Brothers Gin that Mrs. Gaddy referred to. The other likely belonged to T. D. Lawrence, who had a gin and store east of the railroad.[2]

The seven Graham brothers who combined their talents and money to engage in business were the third generation of Grahams to live in Jackson County. The sons of Stephen Jirard Graham and Pocahontas Pistole Graham were

Henry Clay (1852–1904)
John Randolph (York) (1853–1911)
Thomas Jefferson (Tom) (1857–1915)
Nimrod (Bud) (1861–1906)
Nathan (Doc) (1863–1906)
Josephus (Dr. Joe) (1865–1920)
James (Jimmy) (1867–1931)

Graham Brothers Gin still stands just east of the railroad. Main Street makes a big looping curve to the south to go around the several gin buildings, now mostly ruins. It is difficult to realize those buildings once housed a lively and prosperous cotton gin.

There were small gins on some farms before Tuckerman was even a village. Oral tradition has preserved the story of Robert Harvey's gin on his farm near Battle Axe. Robert was the father of Sam, Herbert, and Rosie. The mother of these children, Mary Belle Palmer Harvey, had died and Robert Harvey then married the Widow Kennehorn, who had a small child of her own, a girl named Cora.

Bob Harvey built a cotton gin on his farm. It was a one-mule-power contrivance, but it combed the lint off the cottonseed. The mule was hitched to one end of a long pole and the other end of the pole was affixed to the machine. As the mule walked in a circle around the small gin, the mechanism turned. To keep the mule walking his rounds required some-one's constant attention. Harvey assigned that task to his teen-age son, Sam.

Sam became bored with his job of mule tending and persuaded his little four-year-old stepsister that she could gin the cotton. He placed her on the mule's back, put a switch in her hand to keep the mule's attention, and retired to the shade while little Cora, convinced that she was running the gin, rode triumphant, switching the mule's flank and urging him on.

On April 24, 1903, Sam Harvey and others incorporated the Tuckerman Gin Company and filed their articles of incorporation in the courthouse in Newport in Corporation Record Book A at page 352. The record shows there were thirty-four incorporators but does not name them. S. W. Harvey was the treasurer, owning forty shares; George W. Yelverton was president; R. F. Dunn was vice president; and J. W. Sculley was secretary of the new corporation. By 1913, Harvey had bought out the other shareholders and was the sole owner of the gin, which he sold to A. S. Reigler along with his store.

A family story says that in the final conference with Reigler's father, the elder Mr. Reigler, a merchant and ginner from Walnut Ridge and St. Louis, said, "Yes, Mr. Harvey, I will buy your store and gin. It will be a good business for my son, Arthur, who has just turned 21." Arthur Reigler moved to Tuckerman and ran the store and operated the gin for nearly fifty years. He brought with him his secretary, Rose Smith, a beautiful young woman who soon developed tuberculosis. Arthur made all arrangements for her to go to Colorado and stay at a sanatorium there until she was well. When she returned, they were married and lived in Tuckerman the rest of their lives.

In the Depression years of the 1930s, Reigler was unable to pay his debts largely because his customers were unable to pay him, and he was forced to take bankruptcy. This was not unusual considering the times. What was unusual was that when times got better, World War II brought an air force training camp to Jackson County, the economy revived, and Arthur Reigler repaid every one of the debts for which he had been legally forgiven.

Arthur Reigler was the only Jew in Tuckerman, and although he frequently accompanied his wife to the services at the Methodist Church, he never left the faith of his forefathers. Arthur was one hundred years old when he died in 1993. Rose asked Lindley Smith, president of the Bank of Tuckerman and a member of the board of stewards of the Methodist Church, if there should be some sort of service at the church. Smith replied, "I think the people here would like to pay their respects before his body is taken to St. Louis for burial in the Jewish Cemetery." And so it happened that Arthur Reigler, who had lived most of the twentieth century in the Best Little Town in Arkansas, received a Methodist funeral in a church filled with his Christian friends.

The Planters Gin Company was incorporated in 1920 largely at the instigation of J. W. Lindley. Jim Lindley had ridden into Jackson County in 1874 with a one-dollar bill in his pocket. By the end of the nineteenth century, he had become a large landowner, established the Battle Axe Store, acquired a big herd of cattle, and begun the Bank of Tuckerman in 1903. Lindley had married twice. His first wife was Emma Choate and the mother of Carrie Smith, Lucy Penix, and Ada Dowell. After the death of his first wife, he married Willie Gardner and fathered a fourth daughter, Ruth Williams.

The Planters Gin Company sought to involve a number of cotton farmers. The original stockholders in addition to Lindley were Dr. L. T. Slayden, W. S. Armstrong, F. L. Penix, C. E. Harrison, D. C. Dowell, Dr. K. K. Kimberlin, E. V. Holt, C. E. Penix, and B. F. Hartwick. They elected W. S. Armstrong president and C. E. Penix secretary.

On April 22, 1926, the board of directors met and elected a new director, E. W. Boyce, as secretary of the corporation and manager of the gin, an office he held until his death in 1939. The original corporate minute book in the possession of the author reveals little of the growth of the business during those tumultuous years—the roaring twenties and the Depression thirties—but while other businesses were going broke, the Planters Gin flourished. It expanded its ginning plant, added a feed and seed business, installed a new set of scales that were top of the line, and added a diesel engine more powerful and cleaner than the old coal-fired steam engine it replaced.

More on the Cotton Gin

In the early 1930s the problem with cotton was overproduction and low prices. The *Tuckerman Record* quoted some would-be local poet singing: *"Five cent cotton and forty cent meat; how in the world can a poor man eat."* A response to this problem was the federal government's Agriculture Adjustment Act, which limited the planting of cotton acreage to a fraction of what had been historically planted on a particular farm. If the farmer planted more cotton than his allotment, he was penalized. Acreage was estimated, then actually measured with rod and chain to ensure control of the amount of cotton produced. The government then paid the farmer a calculated sum in cash to compensate him for his loss. The landlord who had previously been paid rent by receiving a portion of the crop was left out of this scheme. It was an emergency tactic, but caused a lot of misunderstanding and hard feelings.

At the same time the federal government was building large dams in the West. Water for cotton farming in Texas, New Mexico, and Arizona caused many farmers to shift their cotton farming operations westward.

Harvest was by hand. The lint from each boll of cotton was picked and put in a long pick sack. Sometimes the sacks were as long as seven feet. The war took much of the labor away from Tuckerman and into the armed services and the factories paying big wages to manufacture planes, tanks, trucks, and ships. The mechanical cotton picker had not been perfected, and women and children picked much of the cotton crop.

By 1960 King Cotton was no longer enthroned in Arkansas. The gins, as an important part of the local economy, began a downward slide.

Reigler's Gin was painted black. It was the first to close. It was hard to get parts for anything from 1941 to 1945 during World War II, and really for some time after that. Reigler's was the smallest of the three gins, and it had become less and less profitable. It stood silent for years after the war before it was finally completely demolished.

Graham's Gin was painted white. It was probably the largest in the space its many buildings covered. The platform where the baled cotton stood awaiting shipment to the compress was to the south of the scale office, and the Main Street to east Tuckerman had to make a wide southern curve before it connected with Hazel Street on the east. Some of the superstitious people who lived east of the gin were reluctant to go by that platform after dark. Harvey Bullock explained this to Foster Dowell one afternoon as he was in a hurry to leave the grocery store. "Ghosts can't hurt you, Harvey," Dowell told him. "I know, Mr. Foster, but they can sure make you hurt yourself," he replied as he hurriedly left.

The Planters Gin was painted red. It was the last gin to begin operation. Cotton was disappearing as a major crop in the 1950s and the other stockholders sold the gin to C. E. Harrison. His son-in-law, Ray Hanley, ran it for a few years before R. S. Rainwater bought it. Buck Hurley bought it from Rainwater and sold it to Charley Sue. The last owner was Stephen Graham, who ginned the final bale.

As cotton vanished as the big crop, soybeans took its place. Zenith Seed Company built a large facility north of the gins on East First Street where the old Crystal Ice Company plant had been. A good many of the Graham family had a large investment in Zenith. Marcus Harris, Bud Graham's son-in-law, who had married May Graham, operated Zenith for several years. The company offered the initial stock to the public, and many local citizens became stockholders in the new company.

During the late 1930s, Nathan Graham built a rice mill on the north edge of Tuckerman. Much of the land east of town that had been considered poor cotton land was discovered to be excellent land for growth and production of rice. Rice grows in a husk. While the combine separates the grain from the slender stalk, the "rough rice" must be milled to remove the tight, brown husk to make it an edible product. The mill stood for many years, but as equipment improved it made economic sense to truck the rice to more efficient and modern mills. The Tuckerman Rice Mill stood idle like the cotton gins.

The old-fashioned gins of the 1930s are long gone. After the invention of the cotton picker, the small gins were insufficient to handle the large round bales of seed cotton that the picker quickly produced. Modern machinery in the field required modern gins to handle the crop expeditiously. Today some of the old cotton gins still stand derelict and deteriorating, grim specters of the busy establishments they were in the 1930s.

The scale house was the gin office, a small building, perhaps twenty feet long. In front of the office was the long platform scale that could weigh a team and wagonload of cotton. The farmer drove on the south end of the scale platform, and from his seat on top of fifteen hundred pounds of seed cotton waited for the scale man on the inside of the office to adjust the scale beam and insert a small yellow carbon paper and white card ticket into a slot in the side of the slider on the beam. With the beam balanced, the scale man squeezed the handles on the slider, thus stamping the gross weight of the load. This system required that later the empty wagon and team had to be weighed again and the empty weight stamped on the same ticket. When the difference was calculated, the amount of seed cotton could be determined. The bale of lint was weighed later at the gin platform. All of these weights gave a reasonably accurate weight of the lint and the seed—both valuable crops.

Most farmers sold their cotton to the gin on delivery. The farmer needed the money, and the gin could write checks they could cash at the store or the bank. In earlier days the gin kept cash money to pay for the cotton. One uneducated farmer brought his money in a paper sack to S. W. Harvey's store. Doubtful that he had been paid correctly, he asked Harvey to count his money.

"How much did they tell you you were supposed to get?" Harvey asked.

The farmer told him the amount he had sold his cotton for.

Harvey tossed the sack up on his grocery scale like he would a piece of ham.

"Well, that is exactly what they paid you," he said.

The farmer went all over town telling everyone that Sam Harvey was so smart he could count money by weighing it on the grocery scale.

There was a door in the south end of the Planters Gin scale office. Standing in that doorway looking south one would see the home of Jake Worthington. He and his wife had one of the best vegetable gardens in Tuckerman. Their granddaughter, Mary Wilma, lived with them. She learned to tap dance listening to the tap dancers on the radio, and would frequently give a recital on the front porch to the music of the radio in the front room.

Inside the office a bench ran around the south and west side of the walls. Depending on the season of the year, the bench was full or empty or somewhere in between. The coal-burning stove set in front of the benches in a 4 x 4 sandbox. The scale beam and desk were on the east side of the office together with the scale man's chair. Along the north was a stand-up desk that held a typewriter and an adding machine. In the northwest corner was a small private office hardly bigger than a telephone booth where files were kept in ledger boxes designed to look like big, thick, orange books. The money safe stood on the floor beneath the shelf of files. The telephone hung on the wall—an orange oak box with the mouthpiece extended on an arm and the receiver hanging on a hook on the side. There was no chair in the private office, and the office was seldom used. On the shelf above the safe was a half-sized Coca-Cola machine, installed there because one of the gin crew kept disappearing each morning to "go to town for a Coke." The other door to that building was opposite the private office in the northeast corner of the building at the north end of the scale platform. It looked out on the big "gin yard" where the loaded cotton wagons stood waiting their turn to get their load ginned off. In the past there had sometimes been disputes about whose turn was next until the gin manager assigned Dee Kennedy to keep a list of each farmer as they came off the scale.

Having weighed his seed cotton, a farmer could drive off the scale toward the gin building. It was a two-story building with a drive-through side on the south where the suck hung down from the upper story. Almost all of the movement of cotton was by forced air. The suck was a long silvery pipe of lightweight metal, the lower half enclosed in the upper half and flexible enough to be moved over the load of cotton from front to back and side to side. A vacuum of air pulled the cotton up from the wagon as the suck man moved the suck around over the load.

Inside the gin on the second floor were the "stands." The number of stands determined the capacity of the gin. A very small gin might have only two stands. The Planters Gin was an eight-stand Continental Gin. Seed cotton carried above the stands was pulled down across the "saws," which pulled the lint free from the seed and sent the lint toward the "press" and the seed to the seed house. This machinery made a tremendous racket. The forced air itself that moved the cotton from wagon to stands to press made a constant howl added to the mechanical noise of the saws as they parted the seed away from the cotton.

Pure lint cotton moved back toward the press. Heavy wood slats made two boxes side by side on a rotating floor. The press boxes faced opposite directions so while the west-facing box was being lined with heavy burlap bagging and strong flat metal ties, the other box was being pressed down and the ties buckled to hold the great pressure in the bale. The ginned and pressed bale was pulled out of the box by the pressman and slid across the floor to the outside platform where it was weighed, tagged, and stood for storage until sold and hauled away to the compress in Newport for further downsizing before shipping to the mill.

In earlier times, a coal-burning steam engine and broad heavy woven belts connecting the power source to the moving gin drove all of this machinery. Later, the steam engine was replaced by a diesel engine, which was much quieter, cleaner, and more efficient. The engine house sat directly behind the two-story gin. The engineer at the Planters Gin was Jake Worthington, who lived across the street from the scale house. The ginner was an old gentleman named Uncle Bill Phillips. He oversaw everything that went on inside the gin itself from the suck to the press. Bob Alexander, known generally as Bob Alec, was the pressman. Bob was a small black man in a perpetual good humor. How a man of his size could move five-hundred-pound bales of cotton with such ease and grace was astonishing. Tom Layton and Fred Mooney worked at Planters Gin in the 1930s.

Wayne Boyce Sr., the manager of the gin since 1926, had become increasingly plagued by rheumatoid arthritis that restricted his hands. In the mid-thirties, he employed Edwin Shaver as assistant manager. Shaver was the son of schoolmaster Wesley Shaver and the brother of Charles Shaver, president of the Bank of Tuckerman. Both Shaver men had inherited the quick minds of their forebears. Edwin was so very popular with the Planters Gin customers and other people in Tuckerman that he was elected mayor of Tuckerman. At that time the duties of the mayor did not interfere with one's day job. People served on public boards, councils, and commissions from a sense of civic pride and public duty. It was just what one did, and that helped make it the best little town.

Wayne Boyce Sr. died in early 1939. F. L. Penix became manager, but Edwin Shaver continued as assistant manager until he also became manager. He and his wife, Wanda, became the parents of eleven children, all but one of whom lived to adulthood and nine graduated from college. Many of these Shavers got graduate degrees, and some made Tuckerman their home the rest of their lives. Edwin continued to manage the gin until up in the 1950s when the gin was sold to R. S. Rainwater from Lawrence County.

At the closing of the sale, Rainwater turned to Shaver and said, "Mr. Shaver, you can stay, but your salary will be reduced fifty dollars a month." Shaver replied, "I have always given an employer two weeks notice before I quit a job, but under your terms I don't believe I can afford it," and he promptly went to work for Wilmans Gin at Diaz.

CHAPTER 18

NEWSPAPERS

Some of the earliest newspaper reports about Tuckerman and its goings-on appear in the *Arkansas Gazette,* the venerable periodical that boasts it is the "oldest newspaper west of the Mississippi." By 1896 Tuckerman had a newspaper of its own when L. D. Smith edited the *Tuckerman Gazette.* It did not appear to have a long life, as there is no trace of it beyond that year.

In 1899 Oscar Franklin Craig and a man by the name of Grant published the *Sentinel.* Oscar was the great-grandfather of Robert Craig, present editor of the *Stream of History,* the official organ of the Jackson County Historical Society. Grant went to Newport, and Craig was the sole editor and publisher in 1900. It apparently ceased publication that year, when Craig went across the river to establish the *Newark Journal.*

The *Tuckerman Sentinel* ran the following story, which was reprinted by the *Arkansas Gazette,* July 1, 1900:

> F. L. Cooper, the well-known painter and paperhanger, was painfully injured by a falling scaffold while at work at the Tuckerman Methodist church Saturday. Also who fell were Foster Dowell and E. A. Graham. The scaffolding was not substantial enough.

Foster Dowell in the 1930s wore a two-inch built-up shoe and walked with a cane, perhaps the result of the falling scaffold.

The valedictory of the *Tuckerman Sentinel* appeared as a classified advertisement in the *Newport Evening News*, September 17, 1900.

> For Sale: the material of the Tuckerman Sentinel for sale cheap. Address O. F. Craig, Elgin, Ark.

Tuckerman was then without a paper until Roy L. Elliott began printing the *Tuckerman Times* in offices over R. F. Dunn's store on Main Street in 1908. It, too, was short lived and was succeeded by the *Tuckerman News*, which consolidated with the *Jackson County Democrat* in 1913 and was published by George Fox until it was moved to Tuckerman by Sparks and Company and published as the *Tuckerman Democrat*.[1]

The *Tuckerman Record* was originated by I. L. Franks on December 21, 1921. He sold the newspaper to Penn Davis and William E. Whaley. Davis bought out Whaley and sold the paper to Alfred N. Johnson. Johnson in turn sold it to J. Edgar Parrott in September 1924. With the Parrotts, newspaper stability had arrived.

The *Tuckerman Record* has survived the ravages of time. In its nameplate it carried the wording "established in 1919," but none of those first six years of the *Record* is extant.

The newspaper office was located on the north side of the ground floor of the Masonic Hall building on West Second Street. The printing press, an old Meilie flat bed, was in the far back recesses of the big room. The linotype and job presses were separated from the front office by an open latticework partition. The front office held Mr. Parrott's desk, filing cabinets, the filed and bound copies of the back issues, and a few office supply items for sale. In later years when J. E. Parrott was justice of the peace, the front office also served as his courtroom.

When the *Record* finally suspended publication and went out of business, all the back issues

Tuckerman Census

Year	Population
1890	150
1900	260
1910	583
1920	778
1930	938
1940	875
1950	1,253
1960	1,539
1970	1,731
1980	2,078
1990	2,020
2000	1,757
2010	1,860

of the paper were given to Tuckerman High School. The Jackson County Historical Society microfilmed every page and placed one copy of the film in the Walton Room of the Jackson County Library at Newport, where it is available for research by the public. The historical society donated a second copy to the Arkansas Department of History for its archives.

The Parrotts were amazing people. Their two children were small when they began publishing the *Record,* John only a baby and Elene not born until January 1926. Edgar had to do most of the work of gathering the news, writing the stories, setting the type, and running the press. He was a man of phenomenal energy. He quickly organized a group of country correspondents to write local happenings of their neighborhood; that is, Dowell's Chapel, Hickory Ridge, the Boyce Farm, Elgin, and Pond Switch. Many of these reports were of who had visited whom, whose cow had a calf, or similar news. These were not the sort of events that city people would highly regard, but they were of tremendous interest and value to the subscribers of the *Record.*

CHAPTER 19

MOVIES

The earliest movies in Tuckerman were shown in a vacant store building on the ground floor of the Masonic Hall. The hall was on the west side of West Second Street almost a block north of the City Drug Store. In the first quarter of the twentieth century, the Masons had been numerous and prosperous enough to undertake the construction of a two-story building. They borrowed money in complete confidence of their ability to repay it in full, but the Depression thwarted those hopes. It was still used for lodge meetings on the upper floor, but for much of the 1930s the ground floor was empty and available for the occasional movie. In the late 1930s Ed Bowen had a grocery store there, which was later operated successively by Charlie Coe, Walter Coe, and even later by Alvin O. "Hub" Hubbard and Bob Coe.

Lynn Graham Thomas remembers seeing movies there. After the movie, a young black man, Joe Ridley Jr., tap danced to the music of the piano played by his mother, Jessie Ridley. The town's leading barber was Joe Ridley Sr. He and his brother, Bishop Ridley, operated their barber-shop in the center of the block between the Masonic Hall and the City Drug Store. Jessie Ridley was a talented woman who played piano at the Colored Methodist Church on Sunday and taught school during the week.

"Mr. Scaggs Picture Show is coming!" was an excited cry heard and repeated by the youngsters. Mr. Scaggs must have been a known person who owned a movie projector but no theater. The then-vacant store building served as his temporary movie house. He showed *Tarzan* to a big crowd sitting on folding chairs hauled in for the event. Many years later, after there were theaters in Tuckerman, Raymond "Rip" Masters took a movie projector to country schools and showed "movin' pictures." This kind of portable entertainment was the subject of University of Arkansas art professor and novelist Donald Harington's acclaimed book, *The Picture Shower*.

Carl Christian opened the first movie theater in Tuckerman in 1939 in an empty dry-goods store on the south side of Main Street between Reigler's Store and the Bank of Tuckerman. Long and narrow, the former mercantile building was perfect for the projection of movies. Christian outfitted it with "opera seats," bare plywood-veneer seats that folded up to the backrest and were separated by wooden arms. He named it the Tuckerman Theater, which was rather redundant since it was the only one in town.

The *Tuckerman Record* on December 8, 1939, carried a front-page story,

> Carl Christian owner and operator announces this week the formal opening of his new Tuckerman Theater on Sunday with a double feature at no increase in price of admission, continuing through Monday showing "Everything on Ice" and "Wolves of the Sea." On Saturday the feature will be "Call of the Yukon."

On December 22, 1939, there was an advertisement on the front page of the *Record*.

> Little Theater Tuckerman—New RCA sound—
> Ginger Rogers in "The Thirteenth Guest"
> Bargain Night ! Thursday 2 for 15 cents.

Carl Christian was a tall, lean, dark-complected man who came to Tuckerman from Star City. He brought with him a talented youngster, Jimmy Davidson. Davidson was the projectionist and an unusually adept youth. Only seventeen when he came to town, Davidson was already a knowledgeable radio engineer, airplane pilot, and photographer. Years later, he and Tom Choate built one of the first Community Antenna Television services on a small scale in Tuckerman and a much bigger one at Batesville. A front-page story in the *Tuckerman Record* gives the date of operation for Choate's Community Antenna as November 13, 1948.

In that pre-air-conditioned day, Christian conceived the idea of an "open-air theater." A vacant lot almost directly across Main Street from his movie house provided a perfect location. All he needed was a ticket booth, a projection booth at the front, and a tall screen on the alley in the rear. The seats were bare benches. In the summer months this open-air arrangement worked very well in the evening when it was dark enough to show the movie. The mosquitoes, however, had a feast.

Johnnie Julian operated a movie theater in an empty building behind Graham Brothers hog lot about where T Rex stands in 2013. The seats were benches and it was cooled, if at all, by a fan. The movies were generally old westerns, but people came to watch and enjoy.

When the "New Theater" was built in the early 1940s, Tuckerman had class A movies. Alice Chapel Graham Mack, known generally as "Miss Alice," had come to Tuckerman from Barren Fork, "in the hills." People in the hills were generally better educated than the local folk from the "bottoms," and many of Tuckerman's teachers came from the Ozarks. Miss Alice came in the first decade of the twentieth century. She boarded for a time at the S. W. Harvey home. After teaching at Tuckerman for a year or two, she got a better job at Swifton and moved. Sam Harvey persuaded his wife, Maude Harrison Harvey, to have a dinner party to which they invited James Graham ("Mr. Jimmy"). Perhaps that was the beginning of a romance, for Miss Chapel subsequently married Mr. Jimmy and their daughter Aileen was born in the home they built where their great-niece, Martha Ann Harris Gilleylen, still lives. Mr. Jimmy died in the mid-1930s. Aileen graduated from Northwestern University, married Joe Masek, and moved to Minneapolis.

Miss Alice wanted to "do something for the young people in town." She considered building a swimming pool, but ultimately decided that a first-class movie theater would be a year-round enjoyment. The building formerly occupied by the Hubert Hanley store next to her home was converted to a movie theater. There was a ticket booth in the northeast corner, a lobby with a popcorn machine presided over by Eugenia Atway, and then the curtained entrances to the theater itself. A new floor was built about three feet above grade. The three sections of seating sloped down to the screen, thus giving the patrons at the rear a view over the heads of the moviegoers down front.

VII.

The Past, Present, and Future

S.W. Harvey home corner of West Second and Harvey Streets about 1905

CHAPTER 20

THIRTIES AND FORTIES

Law Enforcement

The word "Calaboose" is seldom heard in the twenty-first century, but everyone in Tuckerman understood perfectly this southwestern name for the local jail. It stood between the Baptist Church and Tom Caughron's blacksmith shop and gristmill, well back from the sidewalk where children walked to and from school. On the rare occasion when there was an occupant in the little square, flat-roofed, gray concrete prison, the schoolchildren passing along the street kept well to the sidewalk. It was a bleak, grim, and forbidding reminder to obey the law. It must have been hotter than the hinges of Hades in the summer, colder than kraut in the winter. It was no doubt a very good place to stay away from in any season.

A constabulary of one person handled all law enforcement. This person was either elected by vote along with the other town officials or was simply hired by the town council. Most offices were purely honorary and paid no stipend. The town marshal was the exception; he actually got a small salary or fees. However, this inducement finally failed and the council looked to Independence County for a solution to law enforcement. They hired Noah Harris.

Noah Harris might well have been a character from a book. He was tall, lanky, slightly stooped, and he walked with a little hitch in his gait. He was quiet, soft-spoken, and positively fearless. He wore a long-barreled revolver strapped on his hip, western style, and a silver star on his shirt pocket. His badge of office said "Marshal," and all the little children were afraid of this quiet man. Some of the black community called him "Ol' camel-walking Harris," but certainly not to his face. He came with the reputation of having killed a man or two in Independence County while he was deputy sheriff there. That reputation helped him keep order in Tuckerman.

Not long after Harris moved to Tuckerman he had occasion to arrest a black man for some offense. He took him before the justice of the peace, Edgar Parrott, who was also the editor of the *Tuckerman Record* and who regularly held court in the front office of the *Record.* Why the defendant broke and ran is unknown, but the marshal unhesitatingly stepped out of the newspaper office and fired at the fleeing felon, dropping him in his tracks. If the marshal's reputation had been vigorous before, it became iconic after that.

The war and the construction of the airbase brought a new element to Tuckerman. Some of these construction workers were from the North. One of them overindulged in beer at Charlie Guire's restaurant; Mr. Harris was called to take him to jail. Harris was walking the man through the alley behind Graham Brothers' office, headed to the calaboose, when the perp grabbed him; they struggled across the highway to the brick wall of the New Theater. The strong young man was choking the marshal when Mr. Harris managed to get his revolver out of the holster and fire at his assailant. That ended the struggle, and an ambulance took the defendant away to the hospital where he subsequently died. A coroner's jury ruled it "Justifiable homicide."

About a mile south of Tuckerman was a roadhouse, notoriously known as The Bloody Bucket. It had beer, music, and dancing and a much worse reputation than it probably deserved. There had been some fights there, which gave rise to the sobriquet. Paul Yelverton was always given credit for naming it; certainly his Irish wit was capable of inventing such a nickname. The management, which changed from time to time, anxious to keep down too much raucous behavior, hired Mr. Harris for a small fee to come down and stand inside the door and look over the crowd. Since he had no automobile, he walked down the highway to the roadhouse, made his presence known, and after sufficient time had elapsed, he eased out and walked back to Tuckerman. Such was his reputation for peace and order that those brief appearances satisfied the management and kept the peace.

Jake Winningham became the marshal when Mr. Harris retired. Jake was from a large family in the south end of Jackson County extending into the Bradford area. He served during the war years and until he was elected sheriff of Jackson County, and Ansel Hoyle became marshal. It was about this time that the town of Tuckerman achieved enough population to qualify as a City of the Second Class by adoption of an ordinance proclaiming it to be such. Hoyle thereby became the chief of police. The fact that he was the entire police force did not prevent him from being the chief.

For many years the town employed a night watchman. His duty was primarily to be alert to fires in the business district. To make sure that he stayed awake and patrolled the downtown area, there were two punch clocks installed—one at Graham Brothers' Gin office and the other at H. J. Penix's Phillips 66 Service Station. The watchman was required to punch one clock on the hour and the other on the half hour. In the event of fire, he was to sound the fire alarm.

The fire alarm was a siren located atop the tallest building in Tuckerman, the Masonic Hall. It was a two-story brick structure on the west side of West Second Street between Main and Walnut. It made an unearthly sound loud enough to awake the dead, and certainly loud enough to waken everybody in town. Since there was no fire department, a series of signals told everyone generally where the fire was located. One long was downtown. Two short was the North End. Succeeding numbers indicated the east, south, and west sides of town. After 1936 there was a system of fire hydrants all over town and a fire hose and cart. Not until after the war did Tuckerman have a real fire truck.

The fire truck was a project of the Tuckerman Service Club, a group of men who met weekly for lunch at Clausen's Café in the North End. Jim Denton was mayor and a member of the Service Club. A second-hand truck was located, and with the combined efforts of the club and the town, it was purchased.

Tuckerman Census

Tuckerman grew from a few businesses around the depot to a town of several hundred people by the early decades of the twentieth century, but the stock market crash of 1929 and the subsequent Depression took a toll on the town. Downtown Tuckerman consisted of little more than two blocks

Left to right: J. C. Cole, Foster Dowell (owner of City Meat Market), Bud Churchman, Putt Helms, Ralph Moore.

of business buildings. Town Center was the intersection of Main Street and West Second. Of the four buildings at that spot, two were vacant stores. Hubert Hanley's dry-goods store on the southwest corner closed, and much later became the New Theater. The Smith Building, a large two-story brick on the northeast corner, was vacant most of the time, and loafers sat in the embrasure of its west windows. Greenhaw Mercantile, Charley P. Greenhaw, manager, on the southeast corner was the largest store in town; actually, it was two stores with the shoes and clothing on the west side behind a wide tile entryway, and groceries and hardware on the east side. The City Drug Store, distinguished from all the red-brick buildings downtown by its blond-brick façade, flourished on the northwest corner. Hubert Hall, pharmacist, Maurice Livingston, and Hall's son-in-law, Joel Anderson, operated it. Highway 67 and West Second Street were synonymous. Van Smith's wife, Elizabeth, joked that she lived on the only paved street in Tuckerman. Literally that was true, but only because the Smiths lived in the North End on Highway 67, which the Arkansas State Highway Department had paved through Tuckerman in 1933. For most of its length through Tuckerman, the highway was laid on top of West Second Street. At the Baptist Church it swerved to the west because Tuckerman School, the two-story red-brick building that burned in 1944, stood squarely in its due-south path. The town planners had named that terminus street "College Street." It ran only a block before it became Elgin Road and continued west.

Hubert Hanley had bought a lot of surplus army uniforms left over from World War I. They were perfectly good, warm coats, pants, and overcoats, but the army required that the brass buttons with army insignia be removed. Hanley gave some of them to children who no doubt played soldier with them. Ben Treatenberg bought one of the overcoats. Treatenberg was a man of small stature and the overcoat swallowed him. He was a peddler who worked the countryside with his pack on his back selling seeds, salves, seasonings, nostrums, notions, and small gadgets to the country people who sometimes paid him in chickens or eggs. He had a large family of small children. But he kept them fed all during the Depression without ever receiving any of the "Relief" money, food, or jobs.

One Sunday morning the roof of the Treatenberg home caught fire; probably a spark from the chimney landed on the wood shingles. Ben grabbed his oversized overcoat, shinnied up to the roof, and beat out the fire with that old army coat. Both the roof and the coat may have had to be patched after that disaster was averted, but this was the Depression, and people did what they had to do to survive.

Continuing down Main Street on the south side was the First National Bank. Around the walls of the lobby were the portraits of the seven Graham brothers who had founded the bank as a state bank named Citizens Bank. Requirements were steeper for a national bank, and sometime in the 1920s the board of directors upgraded it to federal standards and changed its name. Charley Smith was the banker. He was a man of irascible temperament. One hot afternoon Taylor Dowell from the Graham Brothers' office next door walked into the bank to find only Smith present, and he was down on his knees scrabbling through a huge wastebasket, sweat dripping from his forehead, his glasses held on his head by only one ear piece, and trash paper flying in all directions. He looked up at Dowell and in a voice filled with frustration and rage said, "Taylor, life is just one god damn thing after another."

The Graham Brothers' office next to the bank had the appearance of a bank itself. The lobby with a few chairs was separated from the rest of the room by a counter with cage windows. Behind the counter the books were kept, rents received by Hub Cole, and records were made and updated by Taylor Dowell and his assistant clerk, Gertrude (Gertie) Tims. The Citizens Light & Power Company collected its bills there, as did the Tuckerman Water Works. The president of Graham Brothers Company sat in a chair by the front window where he had a perfect view of all that went on up and down Main Street as well as what transpired in the office. That office building with its pressed-tin ceiling is still extant in the twenty-first century as the Interior Decorating Shop and Rob Penix Real Estate.

A north-south alley marked the middle of the block. The medical office of Dr. O. A. Jamison was immediately to the east. It was a gray concrete-stucco structure that had once been the Bank of Tuckerman. The bank needed a larger building and erected a new banking house and put a strange money safe in the front window. It was presumed that any thief attempting to burgle the safe would have his nefarious activities seen by all and sundry. The bankers were so proud of that large round safe they made it the bank's icon, printing a picture of it on all its checks.

Harrison Brothers Store stood next door. Charlie Harrison and his younger brother, Hubert, ran that general store where the customers bought everything from chocolate candy to mule harnesses. At the back center of the store was a large coal-burning stove around which sat the usual customers and visitors. There were nails in kegs, beans in bins, high-top ladies shoes at least fifty years out of fashion on the wall, canned goods on the shelves, plug tobacco in showcases, and tables of miscellaneous merchandise down the middle of the store.

Landowners who also were storekeepers furnished their tenants credit through their stores, with their account to be paid in the fall from the tenant's share of the crop. Most tenant farming was done on a third and fourth basis—that is, the landlord received one-third of the corn and hay but only one-fourth of the cotton as rent for the land. The tenant furnished the mules, tools, and labor for his share. This was "tenant farming," not to be confused with "share cropping." A sharecropper had no tools or livestock, and furnished only his labor and that of his family. For that labor he was paid one-half of the crop he produced, thus leaving the landlord and the tenant to get a fourth each for supplying land and tools. It was a system devised by an overrun and impoverished South to survive the invasion of the Union army. The landowners had no money. The slave labor was liberated. It may not have been a perfect system, but it worked to feed the South for a hundred years after Reconstruction, a yankee term that might more accurately have been called Destruction and Pillage.

A vacant store stood just past Harrison's, and beyond that was Smith's Drug Store. Ralph Smith was a second-generation pharmacist. His father, Lee Smith, had been one of the earliest druggists in Tuckerman and a man of many talents. Smith's was only half the size of the City Drug Store at Town Center. It was in the day before air conditioning, and the store was cooled in the summer by ceiling fans and cold drinks. James Slaughter, a personable high schooler, worked the soda fountain and sold whatever merchandise was on the shelf. Smith himself frequently performed all those jobs. He graciously permitted Grace Dowell Holt to establish a lending library in a loft space over the pharmacy in the rear of the store. She filled the shelves with books given by local residents and worked as the unpaid librarian with the help of other volunteers. Tuckerman was replete with readers who gave books, read them, and worked at getting others free reading material. It may have been the first lending library in Jackson County.

The store on the corner of Main and Front was Reigler's Mercantile. Arthur Reigler had operated a much larger store on Front Street, which his father bought from S. W. Harvey in 1913. The Front Street store burned sometime in the 1920s and Reigler moved up to the much-smaller store on Main Street. Reigler was the only Jew in Tuckerman, but he frequently attended the Methodist Church with his wife, Rose, whom Reigler had been heard to declare looked just like Joan Crawford, the movie actress. She was a beautiful woman, tall and gracious.

Crossing Main Street to the north side brought one to the building S. W. Harvey and J. N. Hout built in 1916 when Harvey returned with his family from Nashville where he had moved for his daughters to attend college. It was a two-story building with Hout & Harvey's Insurance and Real Estate on the second floor, along with the medical office of Dr. J. B. Ivy. At street level was Ivy's Cash and Carry on the Corner. Ivy stocked a wide variety of fresh and canned goods, which he usually handled by himself; only later did he take on Alfred Parrott as a full-time clerk.

There were a lot of Parrotts in Tuckerman. Before the Civil War, George Washington Parrott had owned a large plantation that ran for miles east of Tuckerman west to Pleasant Grove Cemetery. In fact, some of the Parrotts were buried in the northeast corner of that grave- yard. Wash Parrott also owned a large number of Negro slaves. When the Emancipation Proclamation freed the blacks, they took "Parrott" as their patronymic, and in the 1930s there was Ed Parrott, Bud Parrott, and George Parrott, whose granddaughter became a medical doctor practicing in California, all living in Tuckerman with large families.

The male descendants of Wash Parrott living in Tuckerman were all businessmen. Dewey operated an automobile dealership and garage. Edgar edited the newspaper. Jess owned a store and poultry business on Front Street. Bryan organized the Production Credit Association in Newport, and Joe established a Chevrolet dealership in Conway.

Walter Armstrong built his store next door to the Hout and Harvey building in 1922. The date is set in tiles at the front door of the store W.S.A. 1922. It may have been the last general store to operate in Tuckerman. Armstrong was the son of Robert Armstrong, a woodworker and carpen- ter, who had come south after the Civil War. One of the church pews he built still stands in the Methodist Church suitably memorialized by a brass plaque. He, like his brother-in-law Charlie Harrison, had tenants on his farms that he "furnished" through charge accounts at the store. After his son, Otis Armstrong, retired as president of the Bank of Tuckerman and took over the management of the store, it became W. S.'s habit to sit in the sun on an empty wooden crate tipped back against the show window. He was thus engaged when a customer coming into the store noticed that he was no longer breathing. The old gentleman had peacefully died "minding the store."

A fire later destroyed the building between Armstrong's and the Slayden Building. Dr. L. T. Slayden, a graduate of Vanderbilt University Medical School, a planter, and a businessman, built a large two-story yel- low brick building with a store on the grade level and his medical offices on the upper level. It was a fine building containing a walk-in vault such as a bank would have, and a platform scale in the rear of the store where farm tenants could weigh their wagons of cotton or corn. The store was closed and vacant; the bank vault stood ajar. Only Dr. Slayden's medical office was in use upstairs.

The north-south alley divided the block at that point from the equally vacant Bandy Building to the west. It, like Greenhaw Mercantile, was a doublewide building with a few pieces of farm equipment still in the show windows. Another fire had wiped out the store to the west of the Bandy Building, so only empty space stood between it and the Smith Building on the corner that was likewise vacant.

If one crossed the highway or West Second Street there at the Town Center, the City Drug Store stood on the corner usually full of life and merchandise. The soda fountain and five stools stood on the left just past the cigar case. City Drug served Yarnell's ice cream in five or six different flavors—vanilla, chocolate, strawberry, banana nut, tootie fruity, and an astonishingly rich and golden New York vanilla that surely must have been made in heaven. The fountain coke dispenser stood in the center where plain water and carbonated water spouts were located. Several kinds of ice cream novelties were sold—Big Nick, mostly frozen milk with a thin layer of chocolate, sold for a nickel; Drum Sticks were delicious chocolate cones surmounted with vanilla ice cream covered with chocolate and chopped peanuts. Somewhere behind the fountain was a free-standing Coca-Cola cooler that held assorted bottle drinks—Dr Pepper, Grapette, R.C. Cola, and perhaps a few Nehi drinks of various flavors. It was a hand-numbing experience to fish for the Nehi Orange always swimming in the bottom of the ice-cold box full of melted water and chunks of ice. Two white, round-topped, marble tables accommodated those customers who deigned sit at the counter, partitioned off from the front door by a jewelry case of watches, rings, bracelets, and bangles. At certain seasons, fancy, boxed candy set on top of the case. At Christmastime there were stacks of Whitman's Sampler chocolates with its box printed to look as though it had been needle pointed. Whitman's little pun between the needle-worked "Sampler" and the wide assortment of chocolate candies, which one could "sample" until he found his favorite, has endured over seventy-five years.

Around the walls of the drugstore were patent medicines for every ailment known to man. A particularly vile-tasting laxative named "Syrup of Pepsin" shared shelf space with Groves Chill Tonic for the malaria that came every summer with the mosquitoes. There was Lydia Pinkham's Little Pink Pills for some sort of female distress, and Cubeb Cigarettes that were supposed to relieve resperitory difficulty probably caused from smoking the real tobacco kind.

In the very rear of the store behind a partition was the pharmacy where Hubert Hall compounded, stirred, mixed, and otherwise filled the prescriptions written by one of the five physicians in town. Most of it was in carefully measured liquids poured together and bottled. Some medicine had to be weighed out in powders and folded meticulously in white papers, while others were tamped carefully into the small end of clear gelatin capsules and sealed by the other and larger half of it. All this weighing, stirring, measuring, and mixing kept a pharmacist too busy to sell candy or ice cream, a job done by one of the clerks or frequently a high school boy like Sammy Penix or Wayne Boyce.

Heading north along the highway, next door to the drugstore was the City Café operated by Hub Berkhalter and his wife. The blue plate lunch had three vegetables, a choice of meat, and corn bread or light bread and butter, all for thirty-five cents. The establishment sold several brands of beer, but it was principally an eating place. All the customers were white. Black people were not fed in the main front part of the café, but if it became necessary for a "colored person," the preferred polite term, to be fed, they were served in the kitchen, which was separated from the dining room by a latticework partition. There was seldom a problem getting a seat. Most people ate at home in the 1930s.

Next door to the City Café was the City Meat Market and Butcher Shop, Foster Boyce Dowell, proprietor. Dowell lived on Dowell Avenue about three blocks west of downtown. In summer he wore a hard straw hat. He had one shoe built up three inches, which did not completely avoid a limp nor obviate the necessity for a walking cane. He smoked cigarettes in a long holder, and had a delightful sense of humor. Seeing him walking from his home back to the store, cigarette holder tilted in one direction and hard straw hat in the other while the cane swung jauntily with his stride, made an indelible impression.

By the standard of the twenty-first-century supermarket, the City Meat Market was tiny. The shelves on both north and south sides ran from floor to ceiling full of canned goods while heavy wire bins held fresh potatoes, onions, fruit, and other comestibles. The refrigerated showcase held prepared and butchered meat and divided the front market from the huge butcher block at the rear. Behind the butcher block was a large walk-in freezer where beef and pork carcasses hung from hooks waiting to be cut up into smaller parts for sale. The front of the market was a large show

window holding various items for sale and always a stalk of bananas hanging pointing down. Every denizen of Tuckerman who was assigned to a
tropical country in World War II was astonished to learn that bananas
actually grew pointing up rather than hanging down as they always did in
Tuckerman.

On the north side of the City Meat Market was Ridley's Barber Shop.
It was the largest and most finely appointed barbershop in town. Two
black men, Joe Ridley and his brother Bishop Ridley, were the barbers
while Ofree Johnson operated the two-chair shoeshine stand. A freestand-
ing washbasin that looked like it might have come from an Italian villa
occupied the center of the shop. On the rear was pigeonhole shelving
containing individual shaving mugs, each with the owner's name and usually some additional ornamentation such as scrolls of gold or flowers of
crimson hanging on vines of vibrant green. Beyond the wall of mugs was a
public bath dating from an earlier day when not every home was equipped
with a tub or even running water. A man who had been toiling all week
in the fields could come to town on Saturday, have a hot bath, a haircut,
shave, and shoeshine, all in Ridley's Barber Shop.

The shoe shine man in Ridley's Barber Shop was Ofree Johnson, also
a man of color, who worked at a two-chair station elevated above the floor.
When not occupied with a customer, or working on shoes that had been
left to be called for later, Ofree was frequently to be seen sitting in the shine
chair next to the window. His patrons paid Ofree for his services, and he
in turn paid for his corner by sweeping up and other small jobs around the
shop. Foster Dowell, the butcher shop proprietor next door, finding Ofree
whistling as he swept off the sidewalk, said, "Ofree, you don't ever worry,
do you?" Ofree replied, "No, Mr. Foster, every time I sit down to worry, I
go to sleep."

Joe Ridley's wife was an outstanding, educated, and talented woman
who taught school all week in the East Tuckerman Colored School and
played the piano at the Colored Methodist Church on Sunday.

The building north of Ridley's Barber Shop was frequently vacant.
Dad Armstrong installed a bakery there for a while. It always smelled
of freshly baked bread, and the most fascinating device in the shop was
the machine that sliced the loaves of white bread and wrapped them in
wax paper. Although the products of the bakery were delicious, it was

not apparently a prosperous undertaking and Armstrong soon moved to a smaller building at the north end of the block.

Dr. R. O. Norris's offices were just past the bakery. He required only the two front rooms for his waiting room and private office and treatment surgery. First one and then another occupied the remaining two rooms in the rear. Dr. Harry Dowell practiced dentistry there for a short time before moving on to St. Louis. A beautician rented the space and practiced her art when Dr. Dowell moved. It had been vacant for years when Wayne Boyce converted it to his first law office after the war.

Up the street next door were the medical offices of Dr. Kenneth Knox Kimberlin. Dr. Kimberlin's father, also a physician, had moved his family because he was impressed by the richness of the hardwood timber forests and the profits that were being made from logging. He had located first near Campbell Station, but later moved his daughter, Cora, a schoolteacher, his son and medical partner, and his wife to the thriving nineteenth-century town of Tuckerman.

Beyond Dr. Kimberlin's office was a narrow entry to the stairs leading to the second-floor Masonic Lodge Hall, Tuckerman's meeting place. It was the place where the ladies of the Missionary Society arranged and served a community-wide Thanksgiving dinner. Begun as a fund-raising project, it soon became a local celebration, even drawing people from other churches and from Newport. It was the place where the Tuckerman High School Alumni Society held its annual dinner meeting and entertainment. It was where Tom Choate, once pressed into last-minute service as the speaker for the evening when the programmed speaker failed to show, spoke extemporaneously on the learned topic, "Dick Tracy, the Man." The Junior-Senior High School Banquet was held there, and so was every other town function that required seating for a hundred people or more.

Back on the street level was a vacant store. Charley Coe opened a grocery store in the building before he became postmaster and sold the store to Ed Bowen.

Adjoining the grocery was the newspaper office of the *Tuckerman Record*, owned and operated by Edgar and Idella Parrott. Not only did they publish the weekly newspaper, they operated the town's only job printing shop and office supply store. Parrott was a justice of the peace; the front office became his courtroom when minor miscreants had to be tried or civil disputed resolved. It was a busy and varied place, but no matter its current

function it always had the distinctive, delicious aroma of printers ink about
it.

Someone built a small one-story red-brick building onto the north side
of the two-story Masonic Hall. It was a minuscule diner with stools on the
left side of the counter and the grill on the right. Dad Armstrong ran it,
single-handedly at times, sometimes with a waitress. He made and sold a
five-cent hamburger. It may have been a little thin, but it was meat, and
it included mustard in a full-sized hamburger bun. He also made a ten-
cent burger that had considerably more substance to it. Chili was another
house specialty. The meat may have been scant, but the sauce was hot and
the soda crackers uncounted. Dad's was a hangout place. No matter how
sharp the thrust of a customer might be, Dad always had an adequate
riposte.

The last business on the west side of that block was Henry Penix's
service station, frequently called a filling station. Penix and his employees filled tires with air, crankcases with oil, and hopefully gas tanks with
gasoline. Even though gasoline was only eighteen cents a gallon, most calls
were for "five gallons of gas." J. C. Cole worked there and hated to be told
that he looked like Clark Gable, but he could easily have been the movie
star's double. His brother, James Paul Cole, worked there part of the time,
but his talent for repairing radios, et cetera, got him a job across the street.
A black man, Dewey Russell, drove the "trouble truck." It was a single-
seated Model T Ford with all sorts of tools and patches in the rumble seat.
Flat tires were frequent then. A phone call in distress to the station would
bring Dewey with jacks and wrenches to put the spare tire on and take the
punctured one back to the station for a hot patch. The gasoline pumps
were truly pumps. They stood eight feet tall, and the top two feet were
glass with a metal gallon blade on the side. The pump handle was attached
to the side of the tank trunk and operated with a back-and-forth motion
that sent gasoline up a center pipe to the top of the glass cylinder at the top.
The glass and its gauge made it possible for the buyer and seller to easily
verify the amount of the purchase.

For the dollar gasoline purchase one also got the floor of his car swept
out with a whisk broom and his windshield washed and wiped with a
chamois cloth. Since there were several stations in town, it was the quality
of the "service" that brought the customers time after time.

On the east side of West Second Street between the Methodist Church on the north corner and the two-story Smith Building on the south corner was mostly empty space. One store building opposite the *Tuckerman Record* stood vacant until J. C. Biggers installed an eatery there. He and Dad Armstrong ran a sort of contest to see who could make the biggest hamburger for the least money.

A little farther south on that block, Shorty Lane had a cobbler shop where he half-soled shoes and did other repair work. Lane sold out to Jim Shipley, who continued to operate the business for many years. Shipley's frequent advertisement in the *Tuckerman Record* urged readers to "Stop hiding money in your closet." The ad went on to explain that shoes too worn to wear could be made presentable and useful by bringing them in to the shoe shop rather than spending money buying a new pair of shoes. It was a one-man business, but he was never out of work.

Business was so slow that the merchants all agreed to close up on Wednesday afternoon. Most of them went to the baseball game played in Hays Field at the south end of town. Tuckerman had a good local team. Francis Bush, the engineer for the track and signals of the railroad, was the catcher. Benjy Danvenport, who ran James Store, gin, and farms, played first base. He was a tall, lanky man who seemed to be able to reach halfway to second base without ever taking his foot off the first-base bag. Hamlin Conditt, vice president of the Bank of Tuckerman, played third. Frank Greenhaw was in the outfield along with Henry Lee Tims and his brother Tom from time to time.

There were a lot of little country towns in Arkansas, but Dee Kennedy always claimed that Tuckerman was "the best little town in Arkansas," and no one was ever heard to dispute him. On Saturday when people came in from the farms around town, the stores were crowded and the sidewalks and the wagon yard behind Graham Brothers store were full, but during the week, traffic and sales were slow.

The people in Tuckerman were well educated and well informed about what was going on in the world. It was certainly generally known that Germany was rearming and had marched into the Sudetenland in the deal Neville Chamberlin, prime minister of England, made with Adolph Hitler for "peace in our time." World War I, fought only slightly less than twenty years before, left frightful memories. Nobody wanted another war. Steel helmets from "The Great War," turned into geranium pots, hung on some front porches in Tuckerman. The horrors of gas attacks by the Germans against the Allied troops lurked unforgettable in many memories.

But as Germany marched into Poland in September 1939, England and France declared war on Germany, and Tuckerman people understood they were edging ever closer to being drawn into the fight. The fast victory of Germany over the French and English and the almost miraculous escape of the British army from Dunkirk in May and June of 1940 stirred fear and patriotism in Tuckerman. Only two days before the surrender of France, Congress introduced the first peacetime draft act, known as the Selective Service System, requiring all men to register for military service.

Just as Germany was taking over Europe, Japan was making a strong-armed effort to establish the "The Greater East Asia Co-Prosperity Sphere" with Japan as the dominant nation. The Japanese attack on the USS *Panay* was alarming. Schoolteachers took their classes to see the newsreels of Japanese airplanes firing on the American ship in the Yangtze River near Nanking, China. Generalissimo Chiang Kai-shek was putting up a stubborn defense of his homeland.

In America draft numbers were drawn by lottery from a goldfish bowl, and men began to go off to newly constructed army camps for military training. The term of service changed from time to time, but it was originally twelve months.

Suddenly on December 7, 1941, the town was astonished by the news that the Japanese had bombed Pearl Harbor. Where in the world was Pearl Harbor? Everyone was filled with mixed emotions from dread from the memories of the First World War, the "war to end all wars," to patriotic fervor to defend the country. They were inspired by President Roosevelt's address to Congress the next day, calling the Japanese attack "the day that will live in infamy," and they were eager to do anything to aid the war effort to defeat the enemy.

Opportunity was not long in coming. Washington created a bevy of agencies to marshal the assets of America to arm and fight. Gasoline was rationed. Customers could purchase only a few gallons if you were given an "A" sticker for your windshield and very few more if because of business you rated a "B." Farmers, deemed essential to the war effort, got a "C" sticker, which in high theory enabled them to purchase all the gasoline they needed to produce the food and fiber essential to the war. Tires, which up to that time had been made with natural rubber imported from overseas, were strictly rationed, and people were cautioned "Is This Trip Really Necessary?" by large placards posted in public places.

Sugar and meat were rationed, but this was more difficult to accomplish. Issuing ration books to each family approached a solution. There were red stamps for meat, blue stamps for canned goods, and some other color for sugar—another precious commodity because prior to the war most sugar was imported. Shoes were rationed and hard to find even with the appropriate ration coupon. The shoe shop in Tuckerman did a land office business half soling shoes during the war years.

Everyone, at the governments urging, saved paper, silver, tin cans, and other stuff, much of which never made it beyond the warehouses where it was collected. People even peeled the tinfoil off chewing gum wrappers and made it into ever-growing balls for "Defense." Cigarettes were all but impossible to buy because of the enormous quantity of tobacco sent to the army training camps for the millions of men who were drafted. Civilian smokers sometimes resorted to metal and canvas devices that rolled a reasonably accurate cigarette from papers and loose tobacco, like Prince Albert or Bull Durham.

Leonard Brock may have been the first war casualty. He was radio operator on a freighter in the Atlantic carrying supplies to England when a Nazi submarine torpedoed it and all hands were lost.

The vast industrial machine of America converted from automobiles and tractors to manufacturing tanks, warplanes, and ships to carry the men and materiel across the oceans to the fight. The comfortable belief that those oceans protected the U.S. quickly evaporated as the Japanese attacked Alaska's Aleutian Islands and even dropped balloons with both propaganda and small bombs on the California coast. The Japanese residents, both citizens and aliens, on the Pacific coast were rounded up and confined to hastily built camps far from the ocean. It was doubtless a violation of their constitutional rights, but in times of great perceived danger, rights are frequently ignored.

Only four months after Pearl Harbor, Tuckerman was dumbfounded to learn the U.S. Army Airforce planned to build a training base at Tuckerman to train pilots. The Jones Farm, also known as the Paw Paw Farm, was considered the first choice because it had broad acres cleared of trees. Northwest of Tuckerman, the Jones Farm was nearer Swifton than Tuckerman. Ultimately the base was located at the second choice spot,

Mildred Dorsey Chapel, a few miles southeast of Tuckerman. It still carried the name "Tuckerman Airbase" on all the government papers, until the leaders in Newport got it changed to "Newport Airbase." Whether it was named Tuckerman or Newport didn't keep it from being a great benefit and life changer to both towns.

Almost overnight there was full employment. Even high school boys got jobs unloading lumber for the new hangars, barracks, and other buildings that summer of 1942. Mr. Bowden opened a new store on Main Street in what had been an empty building for a decade. The army was slow to get the name change of the base around to all points, and the first cadets sent to the airbase were given train tickets to Tuckerman. Paul Lacy, who later married Gertrude Graham, and some of his increment arrived at the depot in Tuckerman with no idea where to go. They walked down Main Street to Graham Brothers office where Steve Graham told them where the new base was and put his car and driver at their disposal to get them to their quarters.

Some men came with their wives, and though Newport built houses and apartments, the need for rooms was great. Local people in Tuckerman opened their homes to the service men and their wives, renting their spare rooms to them. One civil engineer came to help with the construction of the base and brought his entire family. He rented several rooms from Miss Alice Graham. He spoke with a slight German accent, and the story went around town that although he was working for the U.S. Army, he was suspected of being a Nazi spy and the FBI was watching him. No one ever saw any FBI agents, but that was the temper of the times. Advertising cautioned everyone to not talk. "A slip of the lip can sink a ship." In a town like Tuckerman, hundreds of miles from the ocean, that admonition seemed pretty farfetched.

The airbase made a permanent difference in Tuckerman. Several local girls worked at the base. Quite a few of the men stationed there married local women and made Tuckerman their home after the war. The population grew during the war despite the number of people who left to work in defense plants or to serve in the military forces. In the decade of the 1940s the population grew by 50 percent.

Main Street Tuckerman circa 1948

CHAPTER 21

TODAY AND TOMORROW

Tuckerman began as an old trail and became a market town. All things change. The Present is that infinitesimal time when the Past and the Future meet. The place that has no history has no future. Looking at Tuckerman today one finds neither the magnificent forest that George Palmer saw back in the nineteenth century, nor the bustling trading center of the twentieth, but a church-school-home town in the twenty-first.

In the first hundred years, there were only three or four churches in Tuckerman, but a recent survey shows there are now more than twice that many. The school that started with a single frame building has grown to a large campus of modern buildings. There are fourteen buildings: classrooms, office, gymnasium, auditorium, and library. The high school alone has a student-teacher ratio of twelve to one. The school, now known as Jackson County School since Swifton and Grubbs were incorporated into the district, is fully accredited by the North Central Association. It has a faculty of seventy-nine qualified college-trained and -educated teachers, forty-two noncertified employees, and a budget of over sixteen million dollars.

The residential sections of Tuckerman have grown. In earlier times, the north end was composed of homes on either side of West Second Street. Many of those houses were situated on wide lots with lawns and trees in front and vegetable gardens in the rear. Today more homes have been built in all directions, while many of the older tree-shaded homes remain. On the west side of town, block after block of modern homes have been built in Bjorkman's Addition and Josephine Graham's Addition. South of Harry Lawrence Curve, homes have turned farmland into residential neighborhoods all the way to Gracelawn Cemetery. The cemetery itself shows the change of the town. The old cemetery had only paths for vehicles. Mildred and Vickie Williams led the town in raising the money to change that. Today the streets are all paved. Since early days, the Pleasant Grove Cemetery Association has collected "dues" from people who had lots there. Since the money was woefully inadequate to pay full-time help, Todd Wright, a nearby farmer, was hired to mow from time to time and the rest was done on "Work Day," when people brought their garden tools and cleaned up their family plots. Today the town maintains the grounds at public expense. East Tuckerman shows the most dramatic change with modern brick homes replacing the old frame houses.

The Town Center emphasizes both the Past and the direction of the Future. Most of the mercantile and office buildings are gone; the railroad depot has been razed; only two or three buildings are awaiting fire or the bulldozer. In place of the old store buildings, there is today an indication of what Tuckerman has become and where it is headed. Two modern new banks serve the town's financial needs. A one-time mini-market has been converted into a sports arena. A modern brick senior center has been built. The city hall containing the growing library stands across Main Street from a three-vehicle fire station and ambulance service.

The spirit that has driven all this change is found in the people of Tuckerman. The people, who in their desire to preserve their history, organized themselves into a historical society, which they named "Trails to Tuckerman." They widened the definition to include all the hinterland of Tuckerman once served by country schools, and made those school place-names part of their mantra; Cooks School, Hickory Grove, Elgin, Upper Goetz, Greenhaw, Pond Switch, Pleasant Grove, Long Creek, Bandy's Chapel, Battle Axe, and Campbell Station all appear around the margin of the society's official letterhead. "Each of those places had a 'Trail to Tuckerman,'" President Tommy Young explained.

T. A. Brown and Ollie Baker Brown, his wife, began talking about some kind of organization like "Trails" with some of their children and friends. Within a short time the interest had grown to the point where it needed to incorporate itself and obtain recognition as a historical society entitled to special tax treatment from the Internal Revenue Service. Six years later in 2013, "Trails" has a membership of over one hundred people, has purchased digital equipment to record thousands of photographs and documents about Tuckerman and environs, established and furnished an office and viewing room, acquired digital equipment to project photographs on a large screen in the city hall, and interviewed on camera over a hundred people about their lives and experiences living in Tuckerman. They raised more money to hire a professional web designer to create a website so all the electronic history could be viewed at http//www.TrailsToTuckerman.com. All of this accomplishment was paid for with dues and donations by Tuckerman people, members of the Trails to Tuckerman.

In Tuckerman, the Past and the Future demonstrate why it is the "Best Little Town" in Arkansas, and very likely anywhere else as well.

Appendix: Charter Members of Trails to Tuckerman

There are 133 charter members of Trails to Tuckerman. The names of these researchers and historians are listed below.

A

Bobby Alcorn
Jeff Atwood

B

Gayle Bailey
Dale Baughn
Ethel Baughn
Bill Biggers
Peggy Biggers
Edward Boyce
Henry Boyce
Sam Boyce
Wayne Boyce
Lou Bray
George "Danny" Brock
Sandra Brock
Debbie Taylor Brown
Garrett Ray Brown
Justin Ryan Brown
Max Alison Brown
Ollie M. Baker Brown
Tom "T. A." Brown Jr.
Gary Browning
L. J. Bryant

Sonny Burgess

C

Brenda Casteel
Jon O. Casteel
John Clark
Bobby Clausen
Tammie Clausen
Dulane Crandall
Dr. Alan William Crawford
Beverly R. Crawford
Billye Crawford
Cindy Cysewski

D

Jamie Darling
Jimmie Darling
Jonita Darling
Justin Darling

E

James Elder

F

Barbara Fields

Jim Fields
Mary Ann Ford
Shirley Fortenberry
Peytina Freer

G

James Gardner
Morgan Gilbert
Martha Gilleylen
Rita Morris Grigsby

H

Anga Henderson
Dewey Henderson
Jerry Henley
Margaret Hise
Phyllis Holmes
Cathy Holt
Sid Holt
J. W. Hulen

J

Annette Jackson
Dorcas Harrison Jeffery
Clayton Crawford Jenkins
Cynthia "Cindy" Marie Jenkins
Mary Ann Crawford Jenkins
Robert A. Jenkins
Sara Elizabeth Jenkins
Catherine Nicole Johnson
Dr. Phil Johnson
Sarah Elizabeth Johnson
Arlene Jones
Ruth Jones
Terry Jones
Larry Jordan

K

Kern Kennedy
Ronnie Koller

M

Shirley Manuel
Helen McCool
Leroy Metheny

N

Charlotte Nagel
Chris Nagel

P

Betty Parr
Jan Paschal
Don Patterson
Bob Penix
Sam B. Penix
Annabelle Provence
Sandra Provence

R

Lisa Riley
Perry Riley
Stephen Roley
Rickey Rowland

S

Ashley Shaver
Cathy Shaver
David Shaver
Wesley Shaver
Haley Shoffner
Bea Smith
Lindley Smith
Michael Smith

Billy Don Soden
Tracey Soden
Bob Stoner
Millie Stoner
Robert Summers

Ronald Young
Ronald Blake Young
Tommy Young

T

Kerry Tharpe
Jimbo Thomas
Lynn Graham Thomas
Steve Thomas
Marietta Thompson
Eddie Tims
Mike Turner

V

Mary Lynn Van Wyck

W

Russell Wagster
Linda Watson
Wanda Wells
Freda M. Williams
Mildred Williams
Tommy J. Williams
Vickie Williams

Y

Amy Young
Brandy Young
Brian Russ Young
Eva Young
Holly Young
Jennifer Ann Young
James N. Young Jr.
James N. Young III
Nancy Young

Notes

Chapter 1

1. Joyce Hudson, *Looking for de Soto* (Athens: University of Georgia Press, 1993).

2. *Narratives of the Career of Hernando de Soto*, 2 vols., ed. Edward Gaylord Bourne (New York: Allerton Book Co., 1922), 1:123–24. See also Gloria A. Young and Michael P. Hoffman, eds., *The Expedition of Hernando de Soto West of the Mississippi, 1541–1543* (Fayetteville: University of Arkansas Press, 1993).

3. Phyllis A. Morse, "Parkin State Park," *Arkansas Archeological Survey* Series 13 (1981): 71.

4. Hudson, *Looking for de Soto*.

5. Morris S. Arnold, *Colonial Arkansas, 1686–1804: A Social and Cultural History* (Fayetteville: University of Arkansas Press, 1991), 5.

6. George W. Featherstonhaugh, *Excursion Through the Slave States, from Washington on the Potomac, to the Frontier of Mexico; with Sketches of Popular Manners and Geological Notices* (New York: Harper Brothers, 1844).

7. Featherstonhaugh, *Excursion Through the Slave States.*

8. Scot Akridge, *Southwest Trail*; www.Encyclopedia of Arkansas History and Culture.net.

Chapter 2

1. Mark Twain, *Life on the Mississippi* (New York: Harper & Brothers, 1874).

2. Goodspeed, *Biographical and Historical Memoirs of Northeast Arkansas* (Chicago: Goodspeed Publishing Co., 1889), 865.

3. Lucille Taylor, "Elgin Scotland Honors Its Jackson County Namesake," *Stream of History* 1, no. 3 (July 1964): 7.

4. For more on the indentured servant, see Wikipedia.

5. This makes the author an eleventh-generation American.

6. Goodspeed, *Biographical and Historical Memoirs of Northeast Arkansas.*

7. Phyllis Boyce, *Stream of History* 20, no. 1 (1983).

8. *Newport Independent*, July 13, 1915.

9. Goodspeed, *Biographical and Historical Memoirs of Northeast Arkansas*, 866.

10. Goodspeed, *Biographical and Historical Memoirs of Northeast Arkansas*, 866.

11. Myrtle F. Gaddy, "Charles Pistole and His Descendants," *Stream of History* 26, no. 1 & 2 (Spring–Summer 1989).

12. Goodspeed, *Biographical and Historical Memoirs of Northeast Arkansas*, 900.

13. Lyman Priest, *Stream of History* 28, no. 3 (Fall 1991).

14. Goodspeed, *Biographical and Historical Memoirs of Northeast Arkansas,* 854.

15. Gertrude G. Lacy, *Stream of History* 29, no. 2 (Summer 1992): 13.

Chapter 3

1. *Arkansas Historical Quarterly* (1947): 371.

2. Encyclopedia of Arkansas History & Culture—Roswell Beebe (1795–1856); Butler Center for Arkansas Studies, Central Arkansas Library System, Little Rock, Arkansas.

3. Weaver B. Cook, "The Emperor Without an Empire: The Story of Roswell Beebe and the Cairo and Fulton Railroad," *Pulaski County Historical Review* 33, no. 3 (Fall 1985): 50.

4. *Arkansas Gazette,* November 15, 1925.

5. *Arkansas Gazette,* July 6, 1855, 32.

6. Cook, "The Emperor Without an Empire," 61.

7. Cook, "The Emperor Without an Empire," 61.

Chapter 4

1. Goodspeed, *Biographical and Historical Memoirs of Northeast Arkansas* (Chicago: Goodspeed Publishing Co., 1889).

2. *Stream of History* 2, no. 3 (July 1964): 3.

3. James Logan Morgan, City Directory, 1880.

4. James Logan Morgan, City Directory, 1888.

5. *Stream of History* 42 (2008–2009): 44.

6. Goodspeed, *Biographical and Historical Memoirs,* 854.

Chapter 5

1. Most of the material about the Methodist Church is from an article by Clara Harvey Dowell in the *Stream of History* 21, no. 4 (December 1984).

2. Dowell, *Stream of History* 21, no. 4 (December 1984): 2.

3. The grandson of L. D. Smith, who built the first church.

Chapter 6

1. A detailed review of the history of the Baptist Church may be found in a series of three articles, "First Baptist Church, Tuckerman, Arkansas, 1894–1994," by Billye Crawford and Hazel Ray Warren in the *Stream of History* 31, no. 3 (Fall 1994); 31, no. 4 (Winter 1994); and 32, no. 1 (Spring 1995).

2. Crawford and Warren, "First Baptist Church, Tuckerman, Arkansas, 1894–1994," *Stream of History* 31, no. 3 (Fall 1994): 2.

3. Crawford and Warren, "First Baptist Church, Tuckerman, Arkansas, 1894–1994," *Stream of History* 31, no. 4 (Winter 1994): 14.

4. Crawford and Warren, "First Baptist Church, Tuckerman, Arkansas, 1894–1994," *Stream of History* 32, no. 1 (Spring 1995): 17.

Chapter 7

1. Raymond Bailey, "Tuckerman Church of Christ and Tabernacle Meetings," *Stream of History* 31, no. 1 (Spring 1994): 14.

2. "A History of the Church of Christ Tuckerman," by Dick Blackford 1994, privately published, a copy has been placed in the Jackson County Library, Walton History Room.

3. Bailey, "Tuckerman Church of Christ and Tabernacle Meetings."

Chapter 8

1. Clara H. Dowell, "A Short History of Tuckerman School," *Stream of History* 26, no. 3 (Fall 1988): 6.

2. Dowell, "A Short History of Tuckerman School," 6.

Chapter 10

1. Clifton K. Meador, MD, "From Med School: Shoes, Window Screens, and Meat," Med School (Medscape from WebMD), April 22, 2004, PMC 1395801.

Chapter 13

1. Arkansas Encyclopedia of History and Culture biography.com. Bob Riley.

Chapter 16

1. Goodspeed, *Biographical and Historical Memoirs of Northeast Arkansas* (Chicago: Goodspeed Publishing Co., 1889), 845.

Chapter 17

1. Myrtle Farmer Gaddy, "Charles Pistole and His Descendants," *Stream of History* 26, no. 1 & 2 (Spring–Summer 1989).

2. Goodspeed, *Biographical and Historical Memoirs of Northeast Arkansas* (Chicago: Goodspeed Publishing Co., 1889), 839.

Chapter 18

1. Jane Allen Goodwin, "The Tuckerman Times," *Stream of History* 16, no. 2 (April 1978): 27.

Bibliography

Akridge, Scot. *Southwest Trail*. www.Encyclopedia of Arkansas History and Culture.net.

Arkansas Encyclopedia of History and Culture biography.com. Bob Riley.

Arkansas Gazette, July 6, 1855, 32.

Arkansas Gazette, November 15, 1925.

Arkansas Historical Quarterly (1947): 371.

Arnold, Morris S. *Colonial Arkansas, 1686–1804: A Social and Cultural History*. Fayetteville: University of Arkansas Press, 1991.

Bailey, Raymond. "Tuckerman Church of Christ and Tabernacle Meetings." *Stream of History* 31, no. 1 (Spring 1994): 14.

Blackford, Dick. "A History of the Church of Christ Tuckerman." Privately published, 1994. A copy has been placed in the Jackson County Library, Walton History Room.

Boyce, Phyllis. *Stream of History* 20, no. 1 (1983).

Cook, Weaver B. "The Emperor Without an Empire: The Story of Roswell Beebe and the Cairo and Fulton Railroad." *Pulaski County Historical Review* 33, no. 3 (Fall 1985): 50.

Crawford, Billye, and Hazel Ray Warren. "First Baptist Church, Tuckerman, Arkansas, 1894–1994." *Stream of History* 31, no. 3 (Fall 1994): 2.

Crawford, Billye, and Hazel Ray Warren. "First Baptist Church, Tuckerman, Arkansas, 1894–1994." *Stream of History* 31, no. 4 (Winter 1994): 14.

Crawford, Billye, and Hazel Ray Warren. "First Baptist Church, Tuckerman, Arkansas, 1894–1994." *Stream of History* 32, no. 1 (Spring 1995): 17.

de Soto, Hernando. *Narratives of the Career of Hernando de Soto*, 2 vols., ed. Edward Gaylord Bourne. New York: Allerton Book Co., 1922.

Dowell, Clara H. "A Short History of Tuckerman School." *Stream of History* 26, no. 3 (Fall 1988): 6.

Dowell, Clara Harvey. *Stream of History* 21, no. 4 (December 1984).

Encyclopedia of Arkansas History & Culture—Roswell Beebe (1795–1856); Butler Center for Arkansas Studies, Central Arkansas Library System, Little Rock, Arkansas.

Featherstonhaugh, George W. *Excursion Through the Slave States, from Washington on the Potomac, to the Frontier of Mexico; with Sketches of Popular Manners and Geological Notices.* New York: Harper Brothers, 1844.

Gaddy, Myrtle F., comp. "Charles Pistole and His Descendants." *Stream of History* 26, no. 1 & 2 (Spring–Summer 1989).

Goodspeed. *Biographical and Historical Memoirs of Northeast Arkansas.* Chicago: Goodspeed Publishing Co., 1889.

Goodwin, Jane Allen. "The Tuckerman Times." *Stream of History* 16, no. 2 (April 1978): 27.

Hudson, Joyce. *Looking for de Soto.* Athens: University of Georgia Press, 1993.

Lacy, Gertrude G. *Stream of History* 29, no. 2 (Summer 1992): 13.

Meador, Clifton K., MD. "From Med School: Shoes, Window Screens, and Meat." Med School (Medscape from WebMD), April 22, 2004, PMC 1395801.

Morgan, James Logan. City Directory, 1880.

Morgan, James Logan. City Directory, 1888.

Morse, Phyllis A. "Parkin State Park." *Arkansas Archeological Survey* Series 13 (1981): 71.

Newport Independent, July 13, 1915.

Priest, Lyman. *Stream of History* 28, no. 3 (Fall 1991).

Stream of History 2, no. 3 (July 1964): 3.

Stream of History 42 (2008–2009): 44.

Taylor, Lucille. "Elgin Scotland Honors Its Jackson County Namesake." *Stream of History* 1, no. 3 (July 1964): 7.

Twain, Mark. *Life on the Mississippi.* New York: Harper & Brothers, 1874.

Young, Gloria A., and Michael P. Hoffman, eds. *The Expedition of Hernando de Soto West of the Mississippi, 1541–1543.* Fayetteville: University of Arkansas Press, 1993.